"I have the privilege of endorsing Hurdman's latest book, *Genesis Uncovered* to anyone who desires a better understanding of the *Book of Beginnings*. Rev. Hurdman's work is well written, well researched and easy to mentally and spiritually digest. To my brother, Mike, I say, 'Well done!' To those contemplating the reading of *Genesis Uncovered*, I say, 'Press on, you won't be disappointed.'"

—Rev. Howard Green,
Pastor, Church of the Nazarene

ENDORSEMENTS FOR *GENESIS UNCOVERED*

"Michael Hurdman states in his introduction to *Genesis Uncovered*, "*My hope is that, as you read, you will often pause and say, 'That is fascinating; I never knew that.*'" As I read the book, I gained a great appreciation for Hurdman's inquisitive nature and why answers to questions such as how God's creation story in *Genesis* compares to similar stories from the Ancient Near Eastern Literature. Hurdman puts the book of *Genesis* in the context of the culture in which it was written and answers such questions as who could the Nephilim be. His resource list contains references to many well-known Biblical scholars. This shows that the book is not just what Hurdman thinks but what scholars have contributed to our understanding of the Book of *Genesis*. In *Genesis Uncovered*, Hurdman communicates Biblical truth in an interesting and inquisitive manner. The book demonstrates why Michael Hurdman is an excellent teacher and why his students enjoy taking classes with him. He goes from beyond what the text says to what does this mean to us and to those it was written. It is a fun and informative book. It is an enjoyable and informative read."

—Rev. Dr. Margaret Dunn
Instructor Mid America Christian University

"After reading *Genesis Uncovered* by Micheal C. Hurdman, I have found a recipe for understanding the book of *Genesis* like no other. Michael has delivered just what he promised. With a dash of seminary-level theological spice combined with a full scoop of practical historical background and contextualization he has created a delectable dish to feast on. I will never read *Genesis* the same as before – from a Western perspective. From now on I have a fresh approach to understanding as the original audience would have understood. Thanks, Mike, for your diligence and masterful conveyance of the Book of *Genesis*. I can't wait for *Exodus*!

—Jon A. Rehbein, M.A. Theo; M.B.A.;
Hospice Chaplain

"Having lived and worked in many cultures around the world this book is a great insight into the Ancient Near East culture and language. Both of which have a great impact on faith even if that faith is different from that culture. Hurdman has given a window into the influences of the ANE in *Genesis*."

—Dr. Sherman Critser

GENESIS
UNCOVERED

MICHAEL C. HURDMAN

dustjacket

Genesis Uncovered / Michael Hurdman

ISBN: 978-1-953285-75-1

Published by Dust Jacket Press

Dust Jacket Press
P. O. Box 721243
Oklahoma City, OK 73172
www.dustjacket.com

Cover and interior design: D.E West – www.emoondesigns.com
with Dust Jacket Creative Services

Printed in the United States of America

dustjacket
www.dustjacket.com

CONTENTS

ACKNOWLEDGMENTS

I'll admit it: when I read a book, I don't usually pay much attention to this section. Nobody really applauds all the people behind the scenes. In team sports, players often give credit to the whole team, but somehow, the water boy and the trainers rarely get mentioned. I don't remember where I first heard it, but there's a saying: *"If you see a turtle sitting on a fence post, you know it didn't get there on its own."* Well, I didn't get on my fence post by myself either.

Where should I begin? That's easy—I thank the Lord for putting me in a position to write this book. If someone had told me fifteen years ago that I'd write a book on *Genesis*, I would have thought they were crazy. Not only did God give me the opportunity to write, but He also guided me in gathering the material, gave me the ability, and helped me at every stage along the way.

Next, I'm deeply thankful for my supportive wife. She never blinked when I told her I wanted to write another book—even after we'd already paid for the publication of two others in completely different genres. She never complained when the money I spent on resources began to rival the GNP of a small country!

Of course, because this book is the result of research, much of the material comes from scholars far smarter than I am.

I'm grateful to all the people who recommended books and resources—there are too many to name.

I would also like to express my appreciation to **Mid-America Christian University**. The privilege of teaching the Bible there has been one of the great blessings of my life. In truth, the teaching became learning—deepening my love for Scripture and shaping much of what is found in these pages.

Finally, I'm reminded of something we used to say when I was a carpenter: *"It's the painters who make the carpenters look good. They caulk and cover all our mistakes."* My painter for this project was Dr. Julie Nance. My sincere thanks go to her—her editorial expertise, thoughtful suggestions, and organizational skills greatly improved this book. She kept me accountable for citing my sources, helped prepare the manuscript for publication, and encouraged me at every stage. More than just an editor, she was a friend throughout the process. She also suggested I thank my little dachshund, Rocky—but I suspect that's because she's an animal lover!

INTRODUCTION

Why write a book on Genesis? It is certainly not due to a lack of existing works on the subject. However, I have several reasons for undertaking this project.

First, most Christian preaching and teaching today focuses on the New Testament, which is understandable—after all, it is there that we encounter Jesus Christ, the One whom Genesis first promises. That means much of the Old Testament is neglected.

Second, while we enjoy many of the Old Testament's stories, much of its content remains shrouded in mystery. I saw the need to remove some of the fog, offering a clearer understanding of the Bible's first book.

Third, I recognized that when skeptics challenge the truthfulness of biblical accounts, especially those concerning our beginnings, many believers struggle to provide satisfying answers. Some stories in Genesis do not easily align with modern scientific inquiry, and rather than engaging with these doubts, many simply reaffirm their belief in the Bible's truth and dismiss such concerns as a lack of faith.

However, the apostle Peter urges us to *"always be ready to make a defense to everyone who asks you to give an account for the hope that is in you"* (1 Pet. 3:15, NASB 1995). When these conversations arise, we are often left feeling unprepared, wishing we had a better response.

I am certain that many books are written that the author planned to write. He or she determined to write on a given topic, and they set out to compile resources and began to write. Much of the material in this book started as part of my duty as an associate professor, teaching undergraduate students the Bible.

Several years ago, I was assigned to teach an introductory Bible course to college freshmen. Given my background, this seemed manageable—I held a master's degree in ministry and had served as a pastor for twenty-six years. Having preached thousands of sermons, I assumed that teaching young people would not present any significant challenges. The course required forty-five hours of lecture material, and I initially believed my education and experience had more than prepared me to meet that demand.

However, as I began preparing, I quickly realized that I needed far more material than I could draw from my own background. Determined to fill the gaps, I immersed myself in reading works by respected biblical scholars. Much of what I read is contained in these pages.The deeper I studied, the more I recognized how little I truly knew. At the same time, I discovered just how fascinating the Old Testament is, and particularly, the Book of Genesis.

I also noticed something surprising: many of the Old Testament stories I had been taught were theologically sound, yet they often lacked historical or textual fullness. What I had learned was true, but there was more in the text than what I was taught. More than once, I found myself saying, *"I've never heard that before."* Additionally, I began to see that passages we often skimmed over without a second thought carry profound implications.

After several years of teaching, I considered pursuing a doctorate in Old Testament studies. However, after much prayer and reflection, I decided to take a self-directed course of study—one that allowed me the freedom to explore without the constraints of a formal degree. Semester after semester, my lecture notes grew, and my concern shifted from having enough material to having far more than I could possibly cover in a sixteen-week course. Through this process, I developed a deep love for the Old Testament.

This journey led me to the final reason for writing about the book of Genesis. Initially, I planned to share my lecture notes for the sixteen-week course of the entire Bible. But as I began writing, I found myself including more and more relevant and fascinating information. As a result, I've narrowed the focus of this work to this one book of the Bible.

The goal is to offer more depth than what is typically covered in Sunday School or most introductory college courses while still being less comprehensive than a graduate-level study of one book, filled with confusing things like linguistic syntax. I have intentionally avoided scholarly jargon that would require a Ph.D. to understand, and I have also omitted many details that those well-versed in the Bible would already be familiar with. My aim is to present the richness of Genesis in a way that is both informative and engaging for the average reader.

I do not claim that this book is exhaustive—far from it. In fact, I am sure that after this book is published, I will come across things I wish I had included. My hope is that, as you read, you will often pause and say, *"That is fascinating; I never knew that."* This journey has deepened my appreciation for Scripture in ways I hadn't experienced before, and I trust it will do the same for you.

I have always believed in the sacredness of Scripture and have read through the Bible many times. Yet, now I read with greater understanding. It's one thing to understand the words on the page; it's another to grasp their meaning as they were originally written. In the past, I often read passages in isolation, missing the connections to other parts of the text. But I have learned to see the Bible as a unified narrative, not a collection of disconnected stories.

N.T. Wright compares reading the Bible to reading a play. It is not merely a series of individual accounts, but a single, cohesive story with a setting, characters, and an overarching plot. To fully appreciate it, we must read it as one grand narrative—one that unfolds across multiple episodes or acts.[1]

I'm reminded of the *Star Wars* movies. The first film released didn't explain how the characters fit into the larger story. It was only in later episodes that we learned how certain characters became significant. Similarly, if we enter a play in the middle, we often find ourselves asking why certain characters are acting as they do. This frustrates those who have been watching from the beginning, and someone must take the time to explain what is happening and why.

If we don't understand the beginning of a story, we can't fully grasp the significance of later events. We may have a general sense of what's unfolding, but we'll miss the depth and meaning that comes from knowing what came before. This is why we need to read *The Uncovering of Genesis*. My goal in this book is to provide context for the biblical text, helping to connect some of the dots so that we can better appreciate the incredible work of God.

The first thing we must understand about the Bible is its purpose. John Walton, in his book *Covenant: God's Purpose, God's Plan*, explains:

God has a plan in history that he is sovereignly executing. The goal of that plan is for him to be in relationship with the people whom he has created. It would be difficult for people to enter into a relationship with a God whom they do not know. If his nature were concealed, obscured, or distorted, an honest relationship would be impossible. In order to clear the way for this relationship, God has undertaken as a primary objective a program of self-revelation. He wants people to know him. The mechanism that drives this program is the covenant, and the instrument is Israel. The purpose of the covenant is to reveal God."[2]

It is my prayer that as you read this book, you will come to see God more clearly and develop a deeper desire to know Him more fully.

I must admit that when I first began this journey, writing a book was not part of my plan. Yet, as I write this introduction, I realize just how deeply the material in these pages has become a part of me. Years ago, I attended a seminar led by a well-known speaker and author who spoke about plagiarism in the pulpit. He humorously remarked, "The first time I use a source, I give credit to the original author. The second time, I might say, 'I read somewhere...' By the third time, I'll probably say, 'I've been thinking.'"

With that in mind, I have spent countless hours reviewing my lecture notes and revisiting my sources to properly credit the information I gathered. However, despite my best efforts, I could not locate all sources, and some I simply do not remember. Consequently, if a citation is missing, you may assume that—at least by now—I have been thinking.

To further aid your study, I have included a list of the sources used at the end of each section. I strongly encourage you to explore these works, as they have significantly enriched my understanding, and I believe they will do the same for you.

It's important to establish some parameters for this book. Again, this is not meant to be a comprehensive commentary on every chapter and verse of Genesis—many such works already exist, tailored to various levels of scholarship. As a result, some passages will be omitted entirely, while others will be addressed only briefly. My goal is not to exhaustively cover every aspect of these texts; entire books have been written by brilliant scholars on many of the subjects to a greater depth than what is explored here.

Rather than offering a comprehensive commentary, we will explore certain nuances of Genesis that are often overlooked. I hesitate to use the word "reveal," but my aim is to highlight details that are not commonly discussed. My primary objective is to spark your interest in the Bible and provide insights that deepen your understanding. A secondary goal is to strike a balance between academic rigor and accessibility. I want this book to be credible enough to engage serious students of Scripture while remaining approachable to the average churchgoer.

We approach the Bible as a grand play—one where this book will not include the climax, as that unfolds in the New Testament. Our focus will remain solely on Genesis. It should be noted that all Scriptures will be from the *New American Standard Bible, 1995*.

If you've ever had an eye exam where the doctor flips different lenses and asks which one is clearer, you know the moment when the right lens brings everything into sharp focus. That is what we hope to achieve in this study. By viewing the text through the lens of the ancient Near Eastern world, rather than through a twenty-first-century Western perspective, we can gain a clearer and deeper understanding of the Old Testament. And since the Old Testament lays the foundation for the New, a proper grasp of the former is essential to fully appreciating the latter.

I will do my best to avoid sermonizing along the way. However, having been a preacher for many years, I ask for your grace if, at times, I get excited, forget myself, and begin to preach.

CHAPTER ONE

Context, Context, Context

I have often heard that understanding the Bible is like mining for gold—it requires effort and persistence before uncovering its true value. I still believe in this principle and emphasize it in the Inductive Bible study class that I teach. That means, before we can fully explore the Book of Genesis, we must first clear away some surface-level issues.

Living in the 21st century gives us a unique advantage. We benefit from centuries of scholarship, archaeological discoveries, and linguistic advancements. However, much of this knowledge has primarily served scholars. What allows us to gain deeper insight into Genesis today is access to more accurate interpretations from these same well-informed sources.

Having those sources available means having information that was unavailable for our understanding of the Bible. Therefore, before we begin our study, I want to offer a disclaimer. First and foremost, let me be clear: I believe the Bible is true from cover to cover. As John Wesley, the 18th-century preacher and founder of Methodism, once said, *"Nay, if there be any mistakes in the Bible, there may as well be a thousand. If there be one falsehood in that book, it did not come from the God of truth."*[1]

That being said, some of the insights in this book may differ from what you learned in Sunday School. Over the years, we have heard many Bible stories, but some of what follows will challenge traditional understandings of those stories. This is not a matter of personal interpretation; rather, these differences stem from significant discoveries made over the past fifty years. Advancements in biblical archaeology have led scholars to reexamine conventional readings of Scripture. As one scholar put it, "The challenge comes when archaeological finds either prove contrary to or challenge biblical and historical accounts. They allow the scholar to revisit his conventional reading of the data and look at things from a new perspective." He goes on to say,

> *"Modern archaeology has become more interdisciplinary in its approaches to study and practice. For example, archaeologists now have formed nomological (the science of law or laws) networks by collaborating with geologists, biologists, chemists, and historians, among others, and many views on the multidimensional perception of artifacts (handmade objects) and sites have emerged, increasing and enriching the interpretation of archaeological evidence. This has brought to light complex historical puzzles, clarifying issues ranging from ancient*

dietary practices to the economic conditions of Biblical times."[2]

In practical terms, this means we have gained a deeper understanding of the ancient Near East (ANE), which, in turn, provides greater insight into the cultural context of the Bible. The more we understand biblical culture, the better we understand Scripture. We now recognize aspects of God's work in the Old Testament that were not fully grasped by the people fifty years ago, and our comprehension of these texts has advanced significantly even in the past twenty years. This shapes the approach taken in this book.

Additionally, while I strongly adhere to a historical-grammatical hermeneutic—interpreting Scripture in light of its historical context and original language—I also incorporate what is known as the Redemptive Movement Hermeneutic. This does not imply that God has "changed" in His thinking or that Scripture is anything less than the authoritative Word of God. Rather, it acknowledges that God, in His pastoral wisdom, meets people and societies where they are within their existing social structures. From there, He gently leads them forward through incremental steps toward a greater moral and theological ideal. This progressive movement within Scripture reveals a God who is willing to work within the tension between an absolute ethical ideal and the practical reality of guiding real people toward that goal.[3]

The Christian community has long sought to interpret Scripture with honesty and integrity. As new information comes to light, our understanding continues to deepen. This is evident, for example, in the way our perspective on the role of women in ministry has evolved. Has God changed? No, but our understanding of His intent has become clearer over time.

Clearer Biblical Context

One of my primary concerns is how the Bible is often criticized as being inaccurate—an issue that arises when it is read through a 21st-century Western lens. The problem with this approach is that the Bible is an ancient document written for an ancient audience. While it was not written *to* us, it was certainly written *for* us. To interpret Scripture correctly, we must read it through the cultural lens of the ancient Near East. This approach is sometimes referred to as understanding *the world behind the text.*

Language is deeply tied to culture, and words can carry different meanings depending on their context. For example, when I was young, we might have described someone as "cool," but that did not mean they had a body temperature below 98.6 degrees. Likewise, to grasp the meaning of Old Testament words, we must consider how they were understood by the Hebrew people for whom Scripture was originally written.

As we journey through Genesis, we will encounter words that can be translated into multiple English equivalents. This has led some to question whether this flexibility in meaning undermines the reliability of Scripture, suggesting that if words can mean different things, then interpretation becomes subjective. A student once asked me, *"If we are free to choose word meanings, how can we be sure the Bible means what it says?"*

To address this concern, let me offer six key guidelines that I have used for determining word meanings in the Bible:

Words in Hebrew, like in any language, can have multiple meanings. For example, in English, the word *bark* can refer to the sound a dog makes or the outer covering of a tree. Similarly, *nail* can describe something hammered into wood or the keratin at the end of a finger or toe.

Context determines meaning. This principle is crucial. For instance, in Genesis 1, animals are created before *adam*, while in Genesis 2, they appear after *adam*. The key to resolving this is understanding the Hebrew word *adam*, which can mean *mankind* (humankind) in Genesis 1, much like the word *animal* refers to a category. In Genesis 2, however, *Adam* is used as the name of an individual. Just as I am an *adam* (a human), my personal name could also be *Adam*. The context clarifies the intended meaning.

We are not free to assign arbitrary meanings to words. Words must be interpreted based on their usage rather than our personal preferences.

The chosen meaning of a word should not alter the core message of the text. While words can have flexibility, their interpretation should not distort the Bible's fundamental teachings.

Choosing one word's meaning over another should not determine orthodoxy or heresy. That is, word choice should align with the broader framework of Christian doctrine rather than contradict it.

Our choice of word meaning will not define our relationship with God. While understanding Scripture accurately is important, salvation is not dependent on resolving linguistic nuances.

> *John Walton suggests that we think of culture as a river, constantly flowing with defining currents. In our modern cultural river, we find concepts such as individual rights, privacy, freedom, capitalism, consumerism, democracy, individualism, globalism, social media, the market economy, scientific naturalism, and natural laws, to name a few. These shape the way we perceive the world. However, the Old Testament was written to people immersed in the cultural river of the ancient Near East (ANE). Their fundamental concerns were vastly different from ours. Instead of individualism, they prioritized community identity. Rather than natural laws, they saw the world as under the complete control of the gods. Central to their worldview were kingship, divination (such as interpreting animal entrails for divine messages), the temple as the heart of religious life, and the ever-present reality of the spirit world and magic.*[4]

What we consider important today was not significant to them, and the issues that consumed their daily thoughts may not even cross our minds. Recognizing these differences is essential for understanding the biblical text in its original context.

In today's world, people may find themselves at odds with certain currents in their cultural river and seek to resist them. However, such resistance is difficult. Even when we succeed in pushing against these influences, we remain within the cultural river—perhaps swimming upstream rather than drifting with the flow.

The same was true in the ancient world. As we read the Old Testament, we see that the Israelites were called to resist certain cultural currents around them. Yet, more often than not, they failed to do so and instead conformed to the surrounding culture.

To truly understand the Old Testament, we must read it within the context of its own cultural river. If we approach Scripture instinctively—without considering its historical and cultural setting—we inevitably interpret it through the lens of our modern worldview. No one reads the Bible free of cultural bias, but we must make a conscious effort to set aside our perspectives and adopt those of the ancient world as much as possible. While we may not always be able to reconstruct the exact worldview of the biblical authors, the first step is recognizing our own cultural assumptions and striving to remove them.[5]

The ANE (Ancient Near East)

When we read the Bible through the lens of its ancient Near Eastern (ANE) culture, one of the first things that stands out is the way people understood deity. The God of the Bible is vastly different from the gods of ancient cultures. Yet, the Israelites did not initially perceive God (Yahweh) as we do today. Instead, they understood Him in ways similar to how their neighbors viewed their own gods. As Scripture repeatedly shows, the Israelites were continually drawn into the religious thinking of the surrounding cultures, whether by adopting foreign gods and practices or by struggling to see Yahweh as truly distinct.[6]

While Yahweh is unlike any deity of the ANE, He communicated with His people using concepts they were already familiar with rather than introducing something radically different all at once. This gradual approach aligns with the Redemptive Movement Hermeneutic, as mentioned earlier. God met the Israelites where they were in their understanding, guiding them step by step until they came to recognize that Yahweh alone is the true God—a revelation that unfolded over time.

When we read the Bible, we often encounter concepts that require cultural understanding, as the text is deeply embedded in its cultural context. For example, consider the phenomenon of *daylight savings time*, which occurs twice a year in much of the United States and in many other places around the world. If someone from a different culture were to hear the phrase "daylight savings time," they might wonder how it is possible to actually save daylight. Simply studying the individual words wouldn't provide the full meaning; they would need additional cultural context to understand the concept. This same problem exists in understanding the ancient text of Scripture.

Another challenge in understanding the Bible is that it was written in what is called *high-context communication*. This type of communication occurs between insiders who share common experiences, values, and assumptions. In these situations, much of the communication can remain unsaid because both the communicator and the audience already understand the context.[7] For an outsider, however, much of this might be unclear. A good example of high-context communication could occur if you were traveling through a large metropolitan city at rush hour, unfamiliar with the area. You might tune into a radio station and hear a traffic report like this:

First stop – Downtown Corridor. We hear reports that Interstate-35 Southbound exit ramp to Cesar Chavez Street is closed due to construction. So far, no major delays, but plan accordingly when heading towards City Center. Keep alternative routes in mind, like the Riverside Drive or Guadalupe Street exits, for added flexibility to reach your destination. Stay safe & keep moving!

Next up, we head to the westside – Highway 290 Eastbound approaching Road 234 is experiencing minor delays near Yager Lane due to lane closures for roadwork. Expect extra travel time and proceed with caution as crews complete improvements to enhance the commuter experience. Don't forget to follow posted signage for detours and alternate paths if needed. You got this; just take deep breaths!

Lastly, we swing by Northeast Austin and focus on Road 620 Northbound between Road 2200 and Road 2187. An accident earlier caused disruptions. While lanes opened fully recently, police activity remains present, so approach slowly.

For you explorer souls willing to venture on scenic routes, why not try Lamar Boulevard or Road 973? The scenery may distract you from being stuck in traffic!

If you're taking public transportation instead, Leander Loop service currently experiences moderate delays, so keep track of schedule updates using the Capital Metro App or website. Remember, bus operators appreciate patience! Thanks for tuning in to our broadcast! Safe drive awaits. Until the next segment – stay cool and travel wisely![8]

If you are familiar with the streets and directions of the city, that traffic report would be incredibly helpful in guiding you home. On the other hand, if you are not familiar with the surroundings, those directions would need considerable explanation to make them valuable to you. Similarly, the Bible was written to an audience who didn't need many things explained.[9] The cultural context was shared, and much of the meaning was inherent in that culture. If we don't understand the ancient Near Eastern (ANE) context, we risk reading our modern cultural assumptions into the text—a mistake that can distort its true message.[10]

Dispelling the Fear of Science

There are two approaches to the relationship between science and the Bible that we should avoid. First, we must steer clear of an anti-science attitude. Science is not the enemy of the Bible, and we should not try to compare the two directly. The Bible is not a scientific textbook, nor does it aim to prove scientific theories. Science deals with repeatable

phenomena, where experiments must yield consistent results to be validated. In contrast, the Bible addresses unique events and the foundational truth that behind everything in creation is a God who set it all in order.

Second, we should avoid the temptation to force a harmony between science and Scripture when they don't align. For example, some people engage in what I call "gymnastic hermeneutics," trying to manipulate the text of the Bible to match scientific claims. This often results in reading into Scripture ideas that aren't there, which can contradict established science. A historical example of this is the 1860s, when Archbishop James Ussher insisted that the world was created in six literal days and that it began at 9:30 a.m. on October 23rd, 4004 B.C.[11] The truth of the Bible does not depend on aligning with scientific theories because its purpose is not to make scientific claims but to reveal God's role in creation and the order He established.

Clarifying Biblical Beginnings

Our Christian Bible is not the original. Before the Protestant Bible as we know it, and before the New Testament existed, there was the Hebrew Bible, known as the *Tanak*. The term *Tanak* is derived from the first letters of the Hebrew divisions of the Old Testament: **T**orah (Law), **N**evi'im (Prophets), and **K**etuvim (Writings). In contrast, our Old Testament is typically divided into sections such as law, history, wisdom literature, and prophecy.

The **Torah**, which is the first five books of the Bible and known as the Pentateuch in Christian tradition, was traditionally attributed to Moses. This raises an interesting question: how can we be sure that Moses' writings about events in *Genesis* are accurate, especially since he wasn't present for any of those events? The answer lies in **oral tradition**.

In our 21st-century Western mindset, we might doubt the accuracy of oral transmission, often dismissing it as unreliable. This skepticism is fueled by experiences like the "telephone game," where a group of people passes a message along from one person to the next, only for the message to be completely altered by the end. We laugh at the result, convinced that oral traditions can't be trusted. However, this perspective doesn't apply to the Middle Eastern cultural context. In that environment, oral traditions were highly valued, and skilled storytellers could accurately pass along information from one generation to the next without error.

We live in a print-based culture, where we rarely memorize anything. One day, my wife had to fill out a form that asked for her phone number. She turned to me and asked, "What's my phone number?" I was surprised that she didn't know it. She replied, "I never call it, so I don't know it."

In contrast, the ancient Near East was a largely illiterate society, and writing was a costly endeavor. As a result, few documents were available for public use. Much of what we have in Genesis was passed down through oral tradition. However, the people of that time didn't just memorize information—they did so within a culture that placed a high value on accuracy and memory. It was a shame-based society, meaning that telling a story incorrectly wasn't just a simple mistake; it was deeply dishonorable.

Kenneth Bailey, in his insightful article *"Informal Controlled Oral Tradition and the Synoptic Gospels,"* offers a perspective that is highly relevant to understanding the transmission of the Old Testament. Dr. Bailey, with his extensive experience in Middle Eastern life, provides valuable insight into how oral traditions were passed down with care and precision in this context. He writes:

> *The formal controlled oral tradition is also a living reality. This form of tradition is most visible publicly in the memorization of the entire Qur'an by Muslim sheiks and in the memorization of various extensive liturgies in Eastern Orthodoxy. Nielsen, in his monograph "Oral Tradition," notes, 'Turning to West-Semitic culture, we remark that it is quite apparent that the written word is not valued highly. It is not considered an independent mode of expression... the written copies of the Qur'an play an astonishingly unobtrusive role in Islam.*[12]

In his famous autobiography, the Egyptian scholar Taha Hussein recounts how, as a young boy of eight, he memorized the Qur'an and also studied *Alflyat Ibn Malik*—a work containing 1,000 Arabic couplets, each defining an aspect of Arabic grammar.[13] Bailey references this example, noting that the esteemed Islamic scholar, Shaykh Sayyed, had these two works completely committed to memory with perfect recall by the age of 75.[14]

Building on Bailey's insights, it's important to understand the Bible as an example of *informal, controlled oral tradition.* Bailey describes a typical setting in which such oral traditions would have been passed down, emphasizing the structure and discipline inherent in the process.

> *The traditional scene is the gathering of villagers in the evening for the telling of stories and the recitation of poetry. These gatherings have a name: they are called haflat samar. Samar in Arabic is a cognate of the Hebrew shamar, meaning 'to preserve'. The community is preserving its store of tradition. By informal, we mean that there is no set teacher and no specifically identified student. As stories, poems, and other traditional materials are told and recited through the evening, anyone can theoretically participate. In fact, the older men, the more gifted men, and the socially more prominent men tend to do the reciting. The reciters will shift depending on who is seated in the circle. I have often been seated in such circles when some piece of traditional oral literature is quoted. I might not happen to know the story and ask what it is all about. Someone then says, 'Elder so-and-so knows the story.' The ranking social/intellectual figure then proceeds to tell the story with pride.*[15]

While there were no official storytellers, only those who had grown up hearing the stories within the community were entrusted with the right to recite them during public gatherings. Various types of material were memorized and retold, but for our purposes, we are particularly concerned with the preservation of historical material.

In the context of informal, controlled oral tradition, the community recites stories that convey a fixed pattern of events. While the overarching sequence of events is constant, and certain words used to express that pattern are fixed, not all words are rigidly prescribed. The storyteller is allowed some flexibility within set boundaries.[16] As Bailey explains, this tradition allows for both flexibility and control, ensuring that the central threads of the story remain intact while still permitting some freedom in how the details are conveyed. What that means is:

> *Continuity and flexibility. Not continuity and change. The distinction is important. Continuity and change could mean that the storyteller could change, say, 15 percent of the story; any 15 percent. Thus, after seven transmissions of the story, theoretically, all of the story could be changed. But continuity and flexibility mean that the main lines of the story cannot be changed at all. The story can endure a hundred transmissions through a chain of a hundred and one different people, and the inner core of the story remains intact. Within the structure, the storyteller has*

> *flexibility within limits to 'tell it his own way.' But the basic storyline remains unchanged.*[17]

He retells such a story and says, "To change the basic storyline while telling that account …is unthinkable. If you persisted, I think you would be run out of the village. They have told [the story] the same way for centuries."[18]

Another consideration when considering oral tradition is that the Bible is not only inspired by God but also safeguarded by His Spirit.

Okay, oral tradition seems reliable, but what about when they started making copies? There were very rigid guidelines for making copies of the text. Josh McDowell, the renowned apologist, tells a story concerning the reliability of copied manuscripts. He writes,

> *"Baruch, it is certified!" Moshe exclaimed as he burst through the door of his friend's home. "I could not wait to tell you." Baruch immediately grasped Moshe's elation, feeling it flood his own heart. Moshe was bringing the news he had been hoping to hear for many weeks now: that the rabbi had certified the Torah (the first five books of the Old Testament) that had taken Baruch a year to painstakingly copy onto a new scroll.*
>
> *His work was eye-straining and back-breaking, as he worked hours on end hunched over a table, slowly and meticulously copying Scripture in a*

room dimly lit by candles or an oil lamp. The scribe undoubtedly followed the strict requirement of preparing the skins and ink, as well as the traditions of precisely copying the Scripture. He certainly was rigorously trained, and highly skilled, a respected religious scholar in his community. To be certified as a scribe, this professional scribe had to memorize 4,000 different laws and principles dictating how to copy Scripture. To begin, the scribe obtained ceremonially clean animal skins from a Jewish butcher, and created the panels for the scroll. Next, he carefully soaked the animal skins in water mixed with his barley leaves. For this particular scroll, he soaked five skins. The soaking softened the skins, making it easier for him to scrape off the hair and fibers.

Then came the critical task of ensuring that he copied every letter clearly and straight. Using threads as guides, the scribe took a dull knife that would not cut through the skin and carefully scored the surface horizontally. This indented the skin slightly to form a distinguishable line. He repeated the same process vertically, creating a perfect cross-pattern grid on which to copy each and every letter of God's written Word.

The scribe believed, like all the Jewish scribes before him, that he had a solemn responsibil-

ity to reproduce every letter perfectly and clearly. Writing his letters on the grid aided him in accomplishing this goal. He knew that miscopying what God said could mean misreading, mispronouncing, and worse, misinterpreting and misunderstanding what God wants his people to know about him and his ways.

In following typical Jewish tradition, this scribe would have dipped his new quill in the freshly prepared ink and uttered each word aloud before he wrote it. "In the beginning..." he would have recited, as he painstakingly formed the letters. But he would have stopped before completing the last letter of the word, just before the word "God." Because, according to tradition, he would need to put down his quill and ceremoniously wash his hands. It was critical to purify himself and sanctify the ink that would pen the name of God.

With 304,805 letters to write — and not a single one allowed to touch another — the scribe's task was daunting. His meticulous care and deliberation is why it took him over a year to complete this very old Torah.

When finally finished, the scribe's manuscript had to be certified as having been transcribed

> *correctly. Some traditions required three separate rabbis to check the accuracy! This meant these persons had to completely unroll this 72-foot scroll to check and count every single word and all 304,805 of the letters. They had to be sure there was the same number of letters in this scroll compared to the Torah from which it was copied.*
>
> *Not only that, when they counted the words, they knew the center word was found in Leviticus 13:33. If the center word of the new scroll did not fall exactly within verse 33, it could not be certified. They did the same thing for every letter. The center letter was found in Leviticus 11:45. If the center letter in the new scroll was in verse 45, they could be confident they had an exact replica of the previous Torah.*[19]

When we apply the same criteria used to judge other historical works, not only is the Bible reliable, but it is more reliable than any comparable ancient writings. Reliability refers to the truthfulness and accuracy of a text, as well as its faithful preservation over time. A text is considered reliable if it is historically and factually correct and if it has been faithfully transmitted through the ages.

To assess the reliability of ancient documents, we often compare the number of copies available and how closely they align with the original. For example, Homer's *Iliad*, written around 900 B.C., has its earliest surviving copy dating to about

400 B.C. There are 643 copies of the *Iliad*, and it is considered to be 95% accurate. In contrast, the New Testament, written in the first century, has copies dating back to the second century, less than 100 years after the original manuscripts. With over 5,600 copies available, it is considered 99.5% accurate. By these measures, the Bible stands as a highly reliable text.[20]

While it is impossible to remove every doubt or obstacle, I hope that I have cleared away some of the debris, allowing for a clearer understanding of the Bible. With that foundation laid, let us now begin our exploration of the book of Genesis.

CHAPTER TWO
Creation

Why is the creation story important to study? It addresses some of life's most profound questions: Who are we, and where did we come from? Were we created for a purpose? Why do we long for relationships? And, perhaps most importantly, what about God? Who is He, and can we have a relationship with Him?

To understand Genesis, we must view it through the lens of the ancient Near East (ANE). The very name *Genesis* means "beginning." Unlike philosophical or theological treatises, the Bible does not attempt to explain God's existence—He simply *is*. Genesis opens with the powerful declaration: "In the beginning, God." He is the First Cause, the Designer, the Originator of all things. Notably, Genesis does not focus on *how* the cosmos was created but rather *why* it was created. The text is not a scientific account but a theological one, revealing the purpose behind creation rather than its mechanics.

When we read, *"In the beginning, God,"* we must place ourselves in the worldview of the ancient Near East (ANE) and how they understood deity. In the ancient world, the gods were believed to permeate every aspect of existence—nothing happened independently of them. The Israelites, like other ancient peoples, saw every event as the direct act of a deity. Every growing plant, every newborn child, every drop of rain, and every natural disaster was attributed to divine action.

Unlike modern perspectives, which rely on natural laws to explain the cosmos, the ANE worldview saw the universe as governed by the will of the gods. There was no concept of *miracles* as supernatural deviations from natural order—only signs of divine activity, whether benevolent or destructive. The gods could bring blessings, but they were just as likely to bring disaster for reasons beyond human understanding.[1] Even today, some people look to the stars for guidance, checking their horoscopes daily—an impulse not far removed from the way ancient peoples sought to interpret the will of the gods.

Other Stories of Creation

Long before the Bible was written, various cultures had their own creation stories. Some have suggested that the biblical creation account was written to refute these myths. While there are clear differences between Genesis and other ancient stories, the Bible's creation narrative is not primarily a polemic against them, nor is it intended as a scientific explanation of how God created the world. Rather, its purpose is to reveal *why* God created the cosmos.

Many ancient creation stories share similarities with Genesis, yet their portrayals of the divine differ significantly.

In Babylonian and Canaanite accounts, creation emerges from conflict among the gods. One of the best-known examples, the *Enuma Elish*, presents a cosmos fashioned from the slain body of a chaos monster, symbolizing a world born from violence and disorder. In this narrative, humanity is created from the blood of a defeated enemy of Marduk, Babylon's chief deity, giving human existence a "demonic" origin.[2]

When we read Genesis against the backdrop of these ancient accounts, we see that it was not intended to provide scientific details about creation. Though it does not directly refute these myths, it offers Israel a radically different understanding of God. Genesis presents Yahweh as sovereign and without rival—distinct from the gods of the surrounding cultures.

In many ancient cultures, the gods had little desire to create humans. However, they required food, clothing, and shelter—and as deities, they expected to be well cared for. Initially, the gods labored to provide for their own needs, but they eventually grew weary of the work. Their solution was to create humans to serve them, supplying food through sacrifices, housing through temple construction, and clothing through ritual offerings. Humanity's primary role was to pamper the gods and attend to their needs.

Because of this dependency, the gods, in turn, had to provide for and protect humans. If crops failed, there would be no harvest, and the gods would go unfed. If enemies threatened a city, the people would be unable to perform their religious duties. If social order collapsed, the well-being of the gods would be at risk. Thus, a mutual dependency formed: the gods sustained humanity so that humanity could care for the gods through ritual and devotion. This dynamic is known as the *Great Symbiosis.*[3]

In contrast, when Yahweh created the world, He did so not out of need or self-interest but to enable humans to live out His image. Unlike the gods of other cultures, Yahweh was entirely self-sufficient and created humanity with purpose, dignity, and a role in His divine plan.

What Is God Doing?

As we consider creation, we encounter the Hebrew verb *bārāʾ*, translated as "create" in Genesis 1:1. But what exactly does it mean? The verb *bārāʾ* appears about fifty times in the Old Testament, and, in the ancient worldview, creation was always seen as a divine act—never something humans could perform.[4]

The details of the creation narrative reveal not just *what* God was making but *what He was doing* in creation. Genesis does not focus on how God merely brought things into existence but on the order and purpose He established. This becomes clear in verse 2: *"The earth was formless and void, and darkness was over the surface of the deep."* This description presents an initial state of chaos.

In the ancient Near Eastern (ANE) worldview, existence was broadly divided into two realms: the ordered human realm, where stability and function prevailed, and the liminal realm, a disorderly space beyond civilization's boundaries. This liminal realm included dangerous animals, barren landscapes such as deserts and mountains, and supernatural threats like demons, wandering spirits, or monstrous beings (Fig. 1).

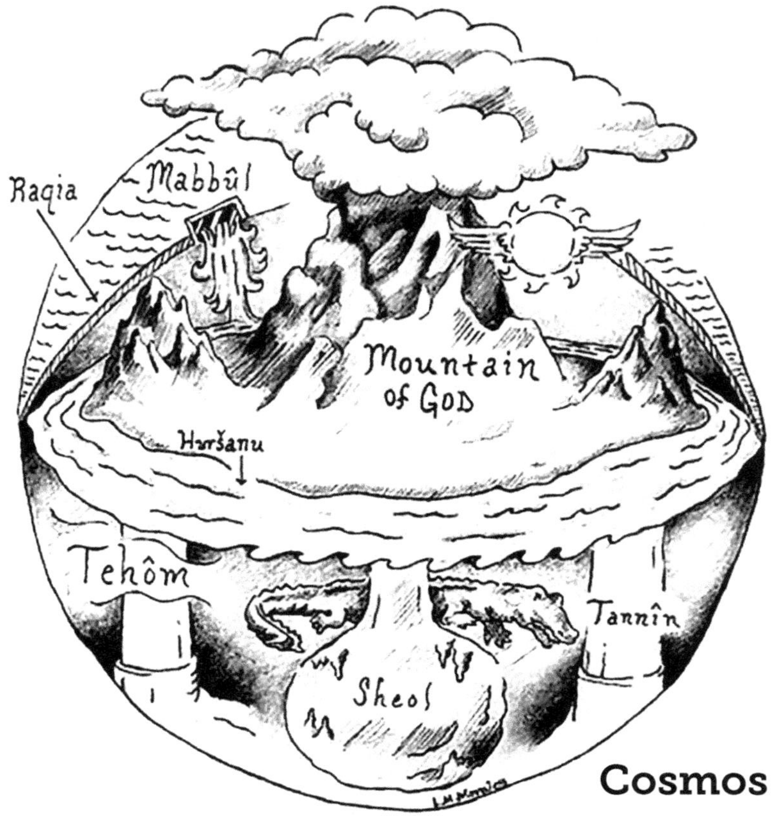

Fig. 1 Hebrew Cosmology

The phrase *"formless and void"* conveys a state of non-functionality—something unproductive and without purpose. Elsewhere in Scripture, the same words are translated as *wilderness* or *wasteland*.[5] Similarly, *"the waters of the deep"* symbolized the primordial chaos that, in the ancient world, represented disorder and the absence of divine structure.

Thus, before God's creative work, the cosmos was in a state of chaos. Over the next six days, He systematically brought order out of disorder. Genesis does not attempt to prove God's existence; rather, it asserts His necessity. Without God, there is chaos; with God, there is order. He is the One who establishes meaning and structure in creation.

This theme echoes in various aspects of life. Consider the laminin protein, a microscopic adhesion molecule that literally holds cells together (Fig. 2).

Fig. 2 The structure of laminin. Image credit: *www.seiyaku.com*

Just as laminin binds our bodies structurally, God's ordering of creation provides stability in the universe. The significance of God creating order extends beyond the physical world—it stands in direct opposition to anxiety and despair. Security comes when our uncertainties are resolved, and our potential pathways converge into a single, clear direction. When we are lost in uncertainty, we experience apprehension—our own form of chaos. Before God's creative act, there was no order. Then, He began to establish it. Even after creation, however, some degree of non-order remained. Outside the Garden of Eden, the world was less ordered, and beyond that lay the liminal realm—a space where chaos still existed.

Sacred Space and the Establishment of Order

In biblical thought, order is closely linked to *sacred space*—the place where God's presence dwells. It is God's presence that brings order and establishes sacred space, making it the center of stability and function. Since God is the source of order, the creation of order is, in essence, the creation of sacred space.

In ancient thought, sacred space was often poetically envisioned as a world mountain surrounded by primeval waters. At its cloud-covered summit stood the temple—God's dwelling place—while at the mountain's base lay the chaotic waters. Beneath these waters was *Sheol*, the realm of the dead.[6] This imagery presents the world as a divinely ordered sanctuary, a place where God's reign is visible and uncontested, sustaining life through His presence. From the mountain's summit, the *waters of life* flowed, symbolizing God's life-giving power.

However, outside the Garden of Eden, the world was less ordered. Genesis 2:15 tells us that God *brought Adam into the garden*, implying that Adam was originally in a less ordered space. This movement toward the garden represents a transition from disorder to divine order. In biblical imagery, moving away from God is often depicted as a descent from the sacred mountain—away from life (creation) and toward death (chaos). Conversely, drawing near to God is portrayed as an ascent—moving from death to life, from chaos to order (Fig. 3).

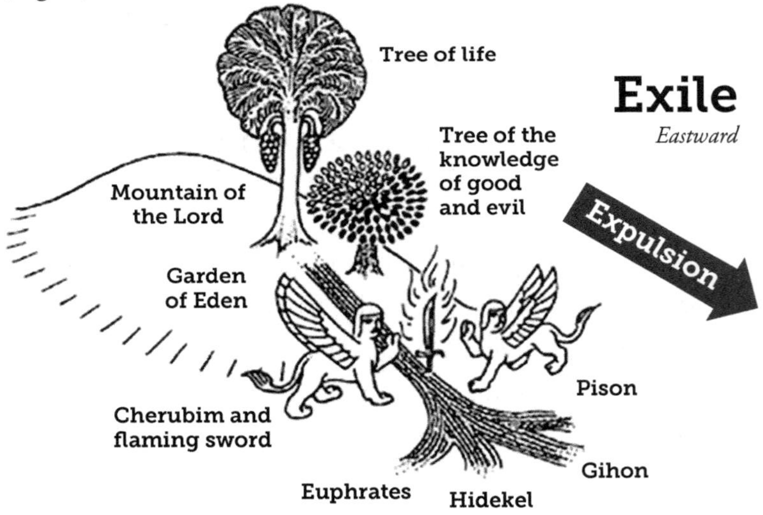

Fig. 3 - Richards, J. K. (n.d.).
Cherubim and a Flaming Sword [Artwork]. Latter-Day Home.

The Garden of Eden, then, would have been understood as resting atop the *mountain of God*. The prophet Ezekiel makes this precise connection when addressing Judah: *"You were in Eden, the garden of God . . . You were on the holy mountain of*

God" (Ezekiel 28:13–14). This description reinforces the idea that Eden was not merely a garden but a sacred space, a divine sanctuary where God's presence brought order and life.

How God Creates

When God creates, He does so *ex nihilo*—"from nothing." The Genesis account reveals that God establishes order out of chaos primarily through *separation.*[7] He separates light from darkness, the heavens from the earth, land from water, and day from night. This theme of separation is central to the creation narrative. In the first chapter of Genesis, the words *divide* or *separate* appear five times, and the concept occurs at least ten more times.

Separation continues to be a significant theme throughout Scripture. God separates Abraham from his family, Israel from the surrounding nations, and Christians from the world. With each act of separation, there is also an act of *naming*. In the biblical worldview, to distinguish something from other things is to bring it into a defined existence; consequently, to name something is to establish its identity. Naming also signifies the ability to relate to what is named and, more importantly, demonstrates sovereignty over it.

We see this divine authority in Genesis 1:5, where God names both *night* and *darkness*. To the ancient Hebrews, darkness was often associated with fear and danger, as nighttime was when evil was believed to be most active. Even the poorest Hebrews kept a lamp burning through the night to ward off uncertainty. Though the text does not state it explicitly, it strongly implies that by naming the night, God is declaring, *"I am sovereign over the darkness."* His authority extends even over the fearful unknown, bringing assurance that He governs all aspects of creation.

Function, Not Form

In the biblical worldview, naming something is not just about assigning a label—it defines its *function*. To name something is to distinguish it from other things and establish its purpose. Consider a room in a house: its function is determined by what it is called and how it is used. A space once designated as a dining room by previous owners can be transformed into a den simply by renaming it and furnishing it accordingly. In doing so, the room's identity is redefined, and in a sense, it is *created anew* as a den.

Genesis reveals that God created the cosmos with a *function* in mind. The recurring theme of *separation* in the creation account highlights this intentional ordering. Each day of creation involves a division—light from darkness, land from water, day from night—establishing distinct roles within creation. This theme of separation continues throughout Scripture: God separates His people from the world, calling them out of darkness into light.

Not only does God separate, but He also *renames*. In Christ, believers are given a new name—they are redeemed, declared *children of God*. Their identity and function are transformed. No longer simply part of the world, they are called to be witnesses, disciples, and servants of the Most High God. Just as creation was given purpose through God's ordering, so too are His people given a new function in His divine plan.

Genesis 1 & 2: Hebrew Cosmology and Functional Ontology

Genesis 1 and 2 present a picture of Hebrew cosmology, which is the ancient understanding of the universe's origin and development. While cosmology today is largely concerned with the scientific study of the universe's material makeup and history, ancient Hebrew cosmology had a different focus. The key difference lies in *ontology*—the way each culture determines what it means for something to "exist."

In modern terms, we think of things in material ontological terms. For example, we say, "The table exists because it has substance." However, in the ancient world, existence was understood in terms of function. The Hebrews would say, "The table exists because we use it to do work." This distinction shapes how the Bible understands creation. When Scripture says that God created, it does not mean He *manufactured* something in the modern sense. We might create a work of art, but we do not *manufacture* the canvas or paint. Similarly, we can create a situation or form a committee. In these cases, to create refers to the *role* or *function* of the thing, rather than its material form.

For example, when we see a computer sitting on a table, we say, "It exists." In the Hebrew worldview, however, the computer would only exist if it were functioning. If the computer has no electricity or programs, it cannot perform its intended function. Therefore, in the Hebrew ontological view, it does not exist because it has no function.

When we read the creation story in Genesis, we are not reading about God creating material objects in the modern sense. Instead, we see God establishing *functions* for His creation. This concept of creating based on function is known as *functional ontology.*[8]

What is Good?

With the idea of *function* in mind, the biblical text repeatedly uses the phrase "it was good" to describe each element successfully placed within its ordered function. The term *good* signifies that the created thing is fully formed and fit to perform its intended work.[9] All the functions described in Genesis are designed for the benefit of humanity. For example, the sun and moon are created to measure time and establish festivals, signs, and seasons that help organize human life.

This functional understanding of *good* is confirmed by the contrast with what is *not good*—for instance, it is stated in Genesis 2:18 that *"it is not good for man to be alone."* This suggests that, according to Genesis, the cosmos cannot fulfill its purpose without the presence of people. The functions of creation are intended for human benefit.[10] God didn't create the world simply to show off His power or because He was bored; He created it for humanity to care for and enjoy.

A helpful analogy can be made to a couple expecting a baby. They prepare the nursery by painting the walls, putting down a new carpet, and purchasing items like a crib, a changing table, and diapers—all for the benefit of the child. In the same way, everything God created was for the benefit of His creatures.

Moses did not write the opening passages of Genesis to address modern concerns about evolution or geological ages. Rather, the purpose of this narrative is to tell us *what* God did and *why* He did it. In doing so, we learn about God's character. We learn that He created for His own enjoyment, seeking a relationship with His creation. We also see that creation is an expression of His sovereignty—God is the Creator, making Him the Lord of all. Yet, in the creation narrative, God's sovereignty is not demonstrated by being served but by serving His creatures.

We also learn that God's character is inherently good, as He creates good things. The order and wisdom displayed in creation reflect this goodness. The world is a complex, well-organized place, with everything designed for a purpose—even mosquitoes. Having served as a pastor in Louisiana for twenty-six years, I've often joked that perhaps God created mosquitoes to keep the "sissies" out of the swamps!

When God created the cosmos, He was making more than just a collection of physical objects. Much like when a couple prepares a nursery for a child, the space they create is about more than just the furnishings. Similarly, God's creation was about preparing a temple—a sacred space where He would rule and dwell with His creation. The cosmos was created as a home, not just for humanity, but for God's presence to dwell.

Why Two Stories?

A common challenge raised by skeptics of the Bible is the apparent contradiction between the two creation stories in Genesis 1 and 2. Some argue that these differences point to errors or inconsistencies. However, rather than seeing these accounts as contradictory, we should view them as complementary. They serve different purposes, and together they provide a fuller picture of God's creative work.

To understand this, consider the analogy of taking two photographs of the same subject. One photo may be taken with a wide-angle lens, showing a broad view, while the other uses a zoom lens, offering a more detailed perspective. The two creation accounts function similarly: Genesis 1 gives us a broad, sweeping view of the cosmos being created, while Genesis 2 zooms in to focus on humanity's creation and relationship with God.

Alexander Desmond, in *From Paradise to Promised Land,* writes,

> *Why are two distinctive accounts of creation found at the beginning of Genesis? By way of addressing this question, we need to recognize that the two descriptions of creation complement each other in a most remarkable way. This is especially so regarding their characterization of the Creator. In 1:1–2:3 God is revealed as separate and distant from his creation. In theological terms, he is transcendent. However, 2:4–3:24 pictures God as very close to humanity, walking and talking with Adam and Eve in the garden. In theological terms, God is immanent. By placing these accounts side by side, the opening sections of*

> *Genesis present a two-sided but complementary view of God. He is both transcendent and immanent. This carefully balanced picture of God is also brought out by the narrator's choice of divine names. In 1:1–2:3 we find repeatedly the designation Elohim (God). However, in 2:4–3:24 the name Yahweh is introduced. Whereas Elohim is the general designation for a deity, Yahweh is a personal name. The use of Yahweh after 2:4 emphasizes the personal nature of God's relationship with humanity, something reflected in the contents of the narrative itself. For this same reason, in 3:1–5 the serpent always refers to God as Elohim and never as Yahweh; as God's archenemy, the serpent refuses to use God's personal name in the presence of Adam and Eve.*[11]

Also, when guests visit your home, they might ask about where you live. However, they are rarely concerned with the plumbing, the air conditioning, or the roof. What they truly want to know is when and how the house became your home. They're not interested in the house's physical construction—they care about its purpose as a space for life and relationships. In the same way, the creation account in Genesis isn't focused on the *how* of the material universe; the fact that God did it is sufficient. The more pressing concern is *why* He created it and *how* it became a home for humanity, a place where God could live with His people. Both Genesis 1 and 2 tell the story of how creation became a home for humanity—and how God prepared it for His own dwelling.

Looking Closer
Day One

Having briefly examined creation from an Ancient Near Eastern (ANE) perspective, let's take a closer look at the days of creation. Day One was likely an exciting time in heaven. The text begins with: *"In the beginning God created the heavens and the earth. The earth was formless and void, and darkness was over the surface of the deep, and the Spirit of God was moving over the surface of the waters. Then God said, 'Let there be light'; and there was light. God saw that the light was good; and God separated the light from the darkness. God called the light day, and the darkness He called night. And there was evening and there was morning, one day"* (Genesis 1:1-5).

This passage does not describe the creation of light as a physical object, but rather the establishment of the cycle of day and night—the creation of the basis for time itself. Notably, light appears before the sun is created on Day Four. In pagan thought, it was inconceivable that life could exist without the sun and its light. As a result, many ancient religions worshiped the sun as the source of light and warmth. The Bible, however, stands apart by declaring that the sun is of secondary importance. Furthermore, Revelation 21:23 describes a future where the New Jerusalem will have no need for the sun, for God's glory will provide light. This suggests that, just as there will be no need for the sun in the future, it's possible that in the beginning, God Himself was the source of light.

Let's now move on to the second day. We will revisit God's assessment of each day in due time.

Day Two

After God has established time, we read: *"Then God said, 'Let there be an expanse in the midst of the waters, and let it separate the waters from the waters.' God made the expanse, and separated the waters which were below the expanse from the waters which were above the expanse; and it was so. God called the expanse heaven. And there was evening and there was morning, a second day"* (Genesis 1:6-8).

In ancient cultures, various explanations were given for the sky's existence. The Egyptians believed the sky was a roof supported by pillars. The Sumerians viewed tin as the metal of heaven. In the Babylonian creation epic *Enuma Elish*, the sky was formed from the body of Tiamat, the goddess of watery chaos. After the victorious god Marduk defeated her, he split her body in half, using one part to create the sky, which he sealed and guarded.

In contrast, Genesis shows God's act of creating the space in which we live and establishing the basis for weather.[12] There were waters both above and below the expanse, and the ancient world believed that rainfall indicated the presence of water above, above the sky itself.

Day Three

On the third day, we read: *"Then God said, 'Let the waters below the heavens be gathered into one place, and let the dry land appear.' And it was so. God called the dry land 'earth,' and the gathering of the waters He called 'seas.' And God saw that it was good. Then God said, 'Let the earth sprout vegetation, plants yielding seed, and fruit trees bearing fruit after their kind, with seed in them.' And it was so. The earth brought forth vegetation, plants yielding seed after their kind, and trees bearing fruit with seed in them, after their kind; and God saw that it was good. And there was evening and there was morning, a third day"* (Genesis 1:9-13, NASB, 1995).

The third day is divided into two main acts. First, God gathers the waters and forms dry land, setting the stage for plant life. Second, He provides the earth with vegetation, which produces seed-bearing plants and fruit trees—ensuring the continuation of life through reproduction. These acts lay the foundation for food production, establishing the means for life to be sustained.[13]

These three functions—time, weather, and food—are the essential building blocks of life. However, the greatest work of the Creator is not found merely in the raw materials He brought together, but in how He arranged them to work together. God didn't just create separate elements; He orchestrated them in harmony, so that they function together for the benefit of humanity.

Day Four

On day four, we read: *"Then God said, 'Let there be lights in the expanse of the heavens to separate the day from the night, and let them be for signs and for seasons, and for days and years; and let them be for lights in the expanse of the heavens to give light on the earth.' And it was so. God made the two great lights, the greater light to govern the day, and the lesser light to govern the night; He made the stars also. God placed them in the expanse of the heavens to give light on the earth, and to govern the day and the night, and to separate the light from the darkness. And God saw that it was good. And there was evening and there was morning, a fourth day"* (Genesis 1:14-19).

On the first day, God created light, setting the foundation for time. On the fourth day, He creates the sun, moon, and stars, establishing the rhythm of seasons. This is not just about distinguishing the natural seasons like summer and winter, but specifically about marking the sacred seasons of the Hebrew festivals. The Hebrew calendar included seven feasts throughout the year, which were linked to agricultural cycles such as sowing and harvesting. God, in His provision, wanted His people to celebrate His goodness through these festivals, emphasizing the joy and community found in His creation.[14]

Day Five

On the fifth day, we witness more separation: *"Then God said, 'Let the waters teem with swarms of living creatures, and let birds fly above the earth in the open expanse of the heavens.' God created the great sea monsters and every living creature that moves, with which the waters swarmed after their kind, and every winged bird after its kind. And God saw that it was good. God blessed them, saying, 'Be fruitful and multiply, and fill the waters in the seas, and let birds multiply on the earth.' And there was evening and there was morning, a fifth day"* (Genesis 1:20-23).

In the ancient world, the cosmic seas were often seen as chaotic forces, representing threats to the ordered system of the universe. The seas were thought to exist in the liminal zone, a boundary between the ordered realm of humans and the unknown, chaotic regions beyond.[15] Yet, in Genesis 1, God demonstrates His sovereignty by creating life within these waters and even commanding creatures to flourish within them. This shows that God controls even the chaotic and seemingly threatening elements of life. The use of the verb *bārā'*, which means "to create," is significant here, as it reinforces the idea that only God can truly create and order these creatures, making them part of His carefully crafted, good creation.

Day Six

Day six marks the creation of animals and humans. In verse 24, we see that the function of animals is to reproduce and fill the earth: *"Let the earth bring forth living creatures"* (Genesis 1:24). Ancient observations suggested that many animal births took place in sheltered environments such as dens or burrows, so it was believed that the land itself brought forth the animals, with babies emerging from the ground.[16]

While we will delve deeper into what it means for humans to be created in the image of God, it's important to note here that Adam's role is intimately connected to the animals, particularly as a shepherd. The dominion that Adam is given is not one of harsh rulership but of caring stewardship, similar to the way Yahweh shepherds His creation.[17]

If we examine the creation days more closely, we see further order emerging. Days one, two, and three form the realms of creation—time, weather, and land—while days four, five, and six introduce the creatures that will inhabit those realms.

When discussing creation with those who may not believe in the Bible's literal truth, it's important to note that while the Bible clearly asserts that God is responsible for all creation—whether functional, material, or otherwise—it does not give a detailed account of material origins. Therefore, we are free to engage with contemporary scientific explanations, such as Young Earth or Old Earth theories, or even the Big Bang theory, as long as we maintain that God is ultimately responsible for the origin of everything. The Bible's primary purpose is not to explain how the cosmos was created, but why it was created.

Having looked at creation as a whole, let's double down on the creation of mankind and what it means to be Human.

CHAPTER THREE
Mankind

There are some notable differences in the details regarding the creation of mankind. In Genesis 1:26, God says, *"Let us create man"*—a personal and relational statement. In Genesis 2:7, we read that God *"formed man"* and *"breathed into his nostrils the breath of life."* This act of breathing into man shows the inherent dignity and uniqueness of humanity. The word for "breathed" and "breath" is the same as the word for "spirit," which indicates that we were created as spiritual beings, setting us apart from the rest of creation.

The idea of being formed from dust doesn't suggest that humanity literally came from dirt. Rather, the Bible is not concerned with providing the ingredients of our material origin, but rather using the image of dust to convey our mortality and destiny. As Genesis 3:19 reminds us, *"Dust you are and to dust you will return."* This serves as a reminder of the transient nature of human life.[1]

Were There Others Besides Adam & Eve?

Did all humans originate from Adam and Eve? While the Bible tells us that Adam and Eve were the first humans, it doesn't necessarily mean they were the only humans. There are also questions surrounding death before the fall and whether Adam and Eve were immortal before sin. What can we learn from Scripture about these matters?

First, the word *"Adam"* appears in two forms. When it includes the definite article, it refers generically to humankind. Without the article, it designates the specific individual, Adam. Thus, sometimes *"Adam"* refers to humans in general, and at other times, it refers to the person.

In the garden, God provided the tree of life. Immortal beings would not need such a tree, suggesting that Adam and Eve were not initially immortal. Their access to the tree was a provision to sustain their life. Once they sinned, they lost access to the tree, and with it, the means to prevent death. As a result, they became subject to mortality.

This also aligns with God's warning to Adam: if he ate the forbidden fruit, he would die. If Adam had no concept of death, why would this warning trouble him? In Genesis 4, we see Cain, the son of Adam and Eve, after murdering his brother, expressing fear that someone would kill him. He says, *"Whoever finds me will kill me"* (Gen 4:14). Who was Cain afraid of? Later, Cain builds a city (Gen 4:17), a term that implies a significant settlement. This suggests that there were likely other people outside the garden who had already experienced death, reinforcing the idea that Adam and Eve were not the only humans.

Thus, death was already part of the world outside the garden, and Adam and Eve were called to continue God's work of bringing order and establishing dominion over creation.[2]

How Long Did Creation Take?

Have you ever wondered if the world was created in exactly six days? The Hebrew word *yom*, which means "day," can also refer to longer periods or epochs. The key point is that God created everything. As always, context is crucial in interpretation.

In Genesis 1:5, we read "light day," indicating a twelve-hour period. The phrase "evening and morning" suggests a 24-hour day. And in 2:4, the text mentions six days of creation. This seems to rule out interpreting "day" as thousands of years. However, when we read the creation account, the author may not have been thinking of 24-hour days, especially since the sun and moon were created on the fourth day. This raises questions about how we should view the timeline.

Creation, however, is not just something that God did in the past. If we think of God's creative work solely as a historical event, it might be easy to overlook His ongoing activity. We've lost sight of the fact that nature doesn't operate independently from God. He continues to create in every baby born, every plant that grows, every cell that divides, and every nebula that forms. While it's easy to marvel at a sunset or the grandeur of mountains, we need to recognize that God's creative work extends beyond these "wow" moments.

We often make the same mistake when we only acknowledge God in extraordinary events in our lives, forgetting that He is present in the everyday, providing for, caring for, and protecting us day by day. God is not just the Creator of the past. He is the Creator—past, present, and future.[3]

Day Seven

There is an interesting contrast between the Hebrew sabbath and other ANE cultures. Certain Babylonian texts prescribe 'evil' days as the 7th, 14th, 21st, and 28th of the month. They warn the king not to eat cooked meat or baked bread, or change his clothes. He must not go out in his chariot or exercise his sovereign powers. Priests were not to deliver oracles, and physicians should avoid touching the sick.[4]

Many have concluded that the sixth day was the culmination and crowning achievement of creation. However, the seventh day is when everything truly finds its purpose. It is the telos, or the end goal, of creation. The question is: What does it mean that God rested?

The word "rest" in this context means "order." When God rested, He was not weary but instead brought order to His creation. In contrast, other cultures often depict their gods resting because they made humans to do the work the gods were tired of. But God doesn't tire, and He is still at work. What He desires is a dwelling place. As Psalm 132:7-8 says, *"Let us go into His dwelling place; Let us worship at His footstool. Arise, O LORD, to Your resting place, You and the ark of Your strength."*

The Hebrew word for rest, "Shabbat" (or Sabbath), means to stop or cease. When God stopped, He declared His creation complete. But this doesn't imply that He is no longer working. It's similar to when someone is elected president of the United States: they take up residence in the White House, not to rest, but to govern the country.

In light of Genesis 1, we can think about the Sabbath in a new way. God's rest on the seventh day involved Him taking up His presence in His cosmic temple. The world had been ordered and made functional, and now He was ready to rule over it.[5] A temple only exists when God's presence is there, and Eden was meant to be that temple.

In the ancient Near Eastern (ANE) worldview, the ordered world was protected and sustained by the gods as they rested in their temples. But this "rest" refers to active residence and rule, not passive relaxation. The gods in these cultures didn't rest in a bed or on a couch; they rested on their thrones, ruling with authority.

When we examine the account of Solomon's temple in 1 Kings 6:37-38, we see that it took seven years to build. Most of this time was spent on the "material phase" of construction: the stone was quarried and shaped, the precious metals mined, the furniture crafted, the cedar acquired and shaped, the veils sewn, the doors carved, the priestly vestments made, and so on. But when all of this was done, did the temple truly exist? Certainly not.

A temple is not merely an accumulation of fine materials or the product of expert craftsmanship. While the temple is constructed from material, it is not itself material. A temple becomes a temple only when the presence of God is within it. If God is absent, it remains just a building. Similarly, if a serving priesthood is not performing rituals, the temple cannot function as intended. Without these elements, it holds no meaning as a temple. It's like a person who only exists as a corpse—without life, they are not truly alive.

It's not the material phase of temple construction that brings the temple into existence; it is the inauguration of its functions and the entrance of God's presence to take up His rest that makes it a temple.[6]

The number seven in the Bible symbolizes completeness. The creation account itself is structured around a Sabbatical principle: it opens with a seven-word sentence, contains seven paragraphs, and climaxes on the seventh day with divine rest. The cycle of time is also marked by sevens. The seventh day of the week is the Sabbath day, the seventh month holds the Day of Atonement (Leviticus 16:29), the seventh year is a year of release from debts and slavery (Deuteronomy 15), and the seventh of seven-year cycles is the Year of Jubilee (Leviticus 25).

Adam Introduced

The tasks given to Adam are inherently priestly in nature: he is entrusted with caring for sacred space.[7] He was to worship God and to guard the garden. For the Hebrews, the priest was essentially a 'guardian' of the temple. He looked after the sanctuary, received visitors, and took charge of their gifts. Aaron's sons were posted in front of the Tent to prevent lay folk from entering. God establishes that this responsibility is too great for Adam to manage alone—he needs an ally to help him fulfill his role within the sacred space. God brings the animals to Adam, and as he reflects on their roles, functions, and names them, he realizes that none of them is his equal.[8]

Eden is often thought to represent a cosmic mountain, with Adam serving as a priest within it.

Behold Eve

Adam's name means "man," while Eve's name means "Source of life" or "mother of the living."[9] In Genesis 2:18, we read, *"Then the LORD God said, 'It is not good for the man to be alone; I will make him a helper suitable for him.'"* Eve was the solution to Adam's deficiency.

I've heard some say that all we need is God, but that isn't entirely true. If all we needed was God, why would He create everything else? He created us to be like Him, and He is relational. As Reuben Welch aptly put it in his book title, *We Really Do Need Each Other.* We need other humans.[10]

Genesis 2:21-23 describes Eve's creation:

> *So the LORD God caused a deep sleep to fall upon the man, and he slept; then He took one of his ribs and closed up the flesh at that place. The LORD God fashioned into a woman the rib which He had taken from the man, and brought her to the man. The man said, 'This is now bone of my bones, and flesh of my flesh; she shall be called Woman, because she was taken out of Man.'"*

What does it mean that woman was created from the side of man? It is an expression of kinship. As Catherine McDowell explains:

> *Kinship in Genesis 1 was expressed as a father-son relationship between God and humankind. In Genesis 2, the theme of kinship is manifest in the relationship between husband and wife. Adam found no suitable companion among the animals, so Yahweh formed woman out of Adam's own body, rather than from the dust of which Adam was made or from the earth from which Yahweh created the animals. This established Eve not only as a fitting counterpart but as Adam's true, biologically related kin, which he acknowledged when he exclaimed, "This time, the bone of my bones and the flesh of my flesh, this one shall be called woman because from man this one was taken."*[11]

The word "woman" carries the idea of a "helper." It could be compared to two boards that lean against each other. This doesn't imply inferiority, but rather that she is his ally—his opposite. She is over against him, complementing and completing him.

There is an equality in creation between man and woman. Eve is described as Adam's helper.[12] But what does it mean to be a helper? What does a helper do? We can look to Psalm 30:10: *"Hear, O LORD, and be gracious to me; O LORD, be my helper."* This certainly doesn't imply that God is less significant than the psalmist. It has been suggested that Eve is a type of savior. In Genesis 2:22, the term *banah* points to the forming of the woman with "artistic skill" as one builds an edifice.[13] God created woman because the task was too great for Adam alone—he needed help.

What are the first recorded words of man? They are about a woman, in verse 23.[14] What does this reveal about human sexuality? Just as in the two creation accounts, man and woman are complementary. They complement each other both relationally and biologically. Since man and woman come from the same root word, she is not given over into his power; rather, she complements him and stands by his side as an equal." The plural form used expresses the public status of the woman. In public or communal life, a woman may appear to be powerless, but this is in the form of a creditor. A creditor loans part of their property or rights in return for something. In this sense, the woman gives up certain rights in public or communal life in exchange for the freedom and time needed to care for her family.[15]

God created humans with distinct roles and functions. The male has a specific role and function, and the female has hers. These roles are not interchangeable. Remember, everything in creation was designed for function. What, then, are the functions of man and woman? We find the answer in Genesis 1:27-28: *"God created man in His own image, in the image of God He created him; male and female He created them. God blessed them; and God said to them, 'Be fruitful and multiply, and fill the earth, and subdue it; and rule over the fish of the sea and over the birds of the sky and over every living thing that moves on the earth.'"*

In these verses, we see that both man and woman are made in God's image and given the charge to steward the earth, to multiply, and to rule over creation. This shared mission reflects their complementary roles in fulfilling God's purposes for the world.

Imago Dei

To understand what it means to be created in the image of God, we must first consider how Yahweh is described. He is portrayed as the sovereign King, ruling by royal decree—"Let there be light"—and presiding over heaven and earth. Humanity is made in His likeness, with the unique role of representing or imaging God's rule in the world.

Just as earthly kings, to assert their dominion, placed images of themselves in distant parts of their empire where they did not personally reside, God places humans on earth as His sovereign emblem. Yet, unlike a despotic ruler, Yahweh's reign is one of service and care. Thus, humanity's rule is not one of tyranny but of shepherding, as humans are called to shepherd and care for all living creatures.

The Hebrew word for "rule" also conveys the idea of controlling land after a military conquest, but it extends beyond domination—it involves guarding and cultivating the earth. Humans are tasked not only with overseeing creation but also with nurturing it. Importantly, while God decrees His will, He also grants authority. Just as He commands the sun and moon to govern the day and night, He invites humanity to participate willingly in His work. Though Yahweh is all-powerful, His commands are invitations to engage in a shared rule with Him.[16]

The Image of God and Ancient Near Eastern (ANE) Cultures

In the ancient Near Eastern (ANE) cultures, people often created cult images or idols to represent their gods. These images were believed to embody the essence of the deity they represented. The idol was not merely a physical representation but was thought to carry the deity's presence and power. The idol did not need to look exactly like the deity; rather, it was understood to function as a medium through which the deity's work was accomplished.

Genesis 5:1-3 draws a parallel between the image of God in Adam and the image of Adam in Seth. This comparison connects the concept of the idol with the idea of human offspring, showing that just as an idol is a representation of its god, a child is a reflection of its parent. What unites these two images is the idea that the image provides the capacity not only to serve as a representative of the deity or parent but also to reflect their likeness. In this sense, humanity is not only a representative of God but also created to be like Him, carrying His essence in the world.[17]

Sandra Richter provides a wonderful understanding of the image from an Ancient Near East culture. She says,

> *Recent scholarship has shed light on a fascinat-*

> *ing practice known as the "Mesopotamian Animation Ritual." Scholars like Michael Dick and Catherine McDowell have explored this ritual, which reveals that ancient Mesopotamians—specifically in Babylonia and Assyria—believed they could animate their idols. These idols were not mere representations but were thought to be incarnations of their deities, brought to life through intricate rituals. The citizens of Mesopotamia worshipped statues, believing that their deities could inhabit these physical forms. They created stunning works of art—crafted by highly skilled artisans—using precious metals like silver and gold and adorning them with jewels. However, the process did not end with crafting the statues.*[18]

Catherine McDowell sheds further light on what transpired in the animation process. She writes,

> *The rituals outlining these procedures and the accompanying incantations are known collectively by the Babylonian titles mīs pî ("washing of the mouth") and pīt pî ("opening of the mouth"). The mīs pî, was primarily a ritual intended to purify the recipient in preparation for cultic activity. As Walker and Dick conclude, "the 'washing of the mouth' was essentially a purification rite which prepared the object/person for contact*

with the divine. It washed away impurities." The mīs pî was performed not only on divine statues but also on the king and his royal insignia, royal statues, priests, individual humans, and various animals and sacred objects. By contrast, the mouth-opening rite (pīt pî) was apparently reserved for inanimate objects, including figurines and larger divine images, a leather bag, cult symbols, and royal jewels. It was thought to consecrate, activate, and/or enliven the object in preparation for cultic use. When applied to a divine statue, the Opening of the Mouth was thought to animate the statue's sensory organs and limbs, enabling it to consume offerings, smell incense, and move freely. Once the mouthwashing and opening were complete, the statue was considered a fully functioning, living manifestation of the divine.[19]

Richter further elaborates,

One critical step in the ritual involved taking the finished statue to a sacred garden, where it was entrusted to a priest. The artisan who crafted the statue would leave and return at dawn the next day. In a ritualized celebration, the community proclaimed, "Behold, the gods have given us a sellum"—an image of themselves. The sacred fiction was that the statue had been divinely birthed in the sacred garden. The animation process involved washing the statue's eyes and mouth in a manner reminiscent of cleansing a newborn baby, who would have had mucus cleared from their eyes and mouth at birth. This is where the ritual gets its name, Mis pi, which means "to wash the mouth." This ritual act symbolized the deity coming to life. Once the statue was considered animate, it was installed in a temple, the dwelling place of the god. To emphasize the divine nature of the statue, the artisans who created it would ritually "cut off" their hands, symbolizing that they had never touched the sacred image. All the tools used to craft the statue were placed inside a sacrificial sheep, which was then cast into a sacred river. This act symbolized the erasure of human involvement, affirming the belief that humans should not create gods—gods should create humans. This ancient practice provides remarkable insight into the theological themes found in the Bible. In Genesis 2, we read that God plants a garden and crafts a human being using the same verb used to describe professional artisans. The human, referred to in Genesis 1 as a sellum—an image of God—is formed as God's divine image. After crafting the human, God breathes the breath of life into this creature, effectively animating him. Then, as in the Mesopotamian ritual, the animated be-

> *ing is installed in the sacred garden, which also serves as God's dwelling place—a temple. This comparison highlights the profound theological statement in Genesis: whereas Mesopotamian rituals involved humans creating images of gods, the biblical narrative depicts God as the artisan, crafting humans as His divine image-bearers.*[20]

Humanity as the Image of God

In many ancient cultures, the gods relied on humans to provide food and offerings to gain favor and prosperity. In contrast, the biblical account shows that it is Yahweh who provides for human beings. While various explanations have been proposed for what it means to be created in the image of God, several key ideas stand out. Some believe that our creativity, rationality, morality, and relational capacity reflect the image of God. Leon Kass writes,

> *Human beings, alone among the creatures, speak, plan, create, contemplate, and judge—and bless. Human beings, alone among the creatures, can articulate a future goal and use that articulation to guide them in bringing it into being by their purposive conduct. Human beings, alone among the creatures, can think about the universe, marvel at its many-splendored forms and articulated order, wonder about its beginning, and feel awe*

> *in beholding its grandeur and in pondering the mystery of its Source.*[21]

The most significant aspect of being created in God's image, however, is our capacity for a relationship with Him. No other part of creation can engage with God in this way.

Additionally, because we are created in God's image, this implies that God is neither male nor female. Both men and women reflect His image, highlighting the equality of all human beings in bearing that image.

Finally, being made in God's image speaks to our potential and purpose. It assures us that our lives have meaning and significance. While Adam and Eve were created as adults physically, they were still spiritually and emotionally childlike, needing to grow in their relationship with God and in fulfilling their purpose on Earth.

Command & Blessing

It is noteworthy that right from the start, we see God giving a command in Genesis 1:28: *"Be fruitful and multiply…"* This command reveals our function as beings created in the image of God. However, it is also a blessing. This is significant—what does it mean that God's command is a blessing? His commands are not burdensome; they are blessings. The very first words God speaks to humanity are words of blessing. In pronouncing this blessing, God affirms our significance, revealing that we are of great value and worth to our Creator.

The word "bless" means to bend the knee, to show honor, and to recognize something as precious.[22] In Genesis, the

word "blessing" appears 88 times in 66 verses, highlighting its importance. Adam, understanding his value to God, recognized that his worth was greater than any other creature. When he looked at Eve, he saw her as of great value to God as well. This sense of value came from God's blessing. God had bent the knee and honored humanity. This insight about how God views creation impacts our self-image, how we treat others, and how we understand the nature of the God we serve.

How did God bless humanity? First, we must consider that they were placed in Eden, which means "delight, pleasure."[23] This context of implies abundance frames the blessing. The command to be fruitful and multiply means that humanity's role is to prosper in the work God has given them. However, there's a distinction between being fruitful and being successful. One can be successful in worldly terms and still be unfruitful. Fruitfulness, on the other hand, is about sustaining life and continuing to produce more. Success is fleeting—it comes and goes.

A fruitful life is not measured by wealth, status, or achievements. It's a mindset rooted in the belief that true fruitfulness comes from remaining in God, allowing Him to grow us and produce good works in our lives. Fruitfulness is not about how much we accumulate, but how much we give and nurture life in others.

Climbing the Right Ladder

I once read, "Too many people would rather climb a trellis than grow a vine."[24] This speaks to the desire to climb the ladder of success rather than climb into the arms of our Heavenly Father. Thomas Merton once wrote, "When you get to the top of the ladder, you may find it is propped against the wrong wall."[25] This warning reminds us that worldly success, if sought above all else, may ultimately lead to emptiness.

In an agricultural society, the success of the fall crop meant survival, while a failed crop could lead to starvation. We need to remember that in the ancient culture of the Bible, blessing was closely tied to fertility and prosperity. Infertility or a lack of produce was seen as a curse, often equated with death. Blessings included more than just material wealth—they encompassed fertility, security, health, peace, shelter, food, freedom from disease, and protection from violence. These blessings were not simply seen as rewards for hard work but as the gracious gifts of God.

In the original plan for humanity, Adam was tasked with filling the earth with people who reflected the same blessings he had received. This was the intent God had for the world: a flourishing, blessed humanity.

Subdue the Earth

In addition to being fruitful and multiplying, Adam was also given the command to subdue the earth. This often comes up in discussions about conservation and environmental responsibility. To "subdue" the earth means not to exploit it, but to exercise sovereignty over it. However, true sovereignty is found in serving. The idea is not to plunder the earth's resources for selfish gain but to care for it, manage it wisely, and protect it. To subdue the earth is to bring it into order, aligning it with God's original plan for flourishing life.

Ruling the Earth

Thirdly, Adam was called to rule the planet. It's important to remember that we are talking about a kingdom, with God as the ultimate King, and humanity was given the task of ruling under Him. This divine mandate was part of the broader blessing that encompassed every aspect of life. It wasn't just about religious observance, but the blessing in the Bible represents the fullness of life—flourishing in every sense.

As we continue through the Bible, we see this blessing passed down through generations: God blesses Abraham, who in turn blesses Isaac, and Isaac blesses Jacob, and so on. This isn't just a transfer of material wealth or power; it's the passing on of the fullness of life—God's divine favor and His intention for humanity to thrive, multiply, and steward the earth.

Imagining Eden

When we read our Bibles using our imagination, it's hard not to wonder what life in Eden must have been like. Eden is often described as a sacred space, a place where God would dwell with man. What made it sacred was not the land itself, but the presence of God.

The Garden of Eden, as described by the author of Genesis, was not simply a piece of Mesopotamian farmland—it was a type of sanctuary. A sanctuary is a holy place where God resides and where humanity is meant to worship Him. Many of the features of Eden are mirrored in later sanctuaries, particularly the Tabernacle and the Jerusalem temple. These similarities suggest that Eden itself was understood as a prototype for the sacred spaces that would follow.

If you've ever walked into a grand cathedral, you can likely recall the feeling of entering a holy place. Churches often have a space called the "sanctuary," which is set apart from the rest of the building. It is not like other places—it is sacred, to be treated with reverence. In a similar way, God created Eden as a sacred space, where He would walk and commune with humanity. Sandra Richter offers valuable insight into this idea, helping us understand that the garden's holiness wasn't just in its beauty or its bounty, but in the divine presence that made it special. Once again, Sandra Richter provides great insight. She said,

> *Here, we learn that sacred space in Israel's world was never chosen simply for convenience or preference. Sacred space was the choice of the gods, and in Israel's case, the choice of the one, true God. The place was typically determined by some sort of manifestation of the god's presence—his activity, his appearance, or his directive. A biblical example of how this played out is when Israel enters Canaan, they are to dismantle the cult sites of the Canaanites, and replace those multiple sites with the one and only site of Yahweh. Why one site? To help them hang onto the idea*

that there is only one God. What did the ancients believe about these sacred sites? They believed that they could meet God there. That this place was the omphalos of the universe—a fancy word for "belly button." Like a "belly button," the sacred precinct was that spot where heaven met earth, where the umbilical cord of the cosmos ushered divine power into human space. For the Israelites, this meant that the Tabernacle in the wilderness, or the Jerusalem temple, was the one place where a worshiper could be assured of encountering the Almighty. Why were these sites holy? Because God was there. And just as the Hebrew cosmology is marked by sacred rivers (which bring fertility to the earth), sacred trees, and a mountain, they all helped to mark the space as one where worship should occur. And if Israel destroys the cult sites of the surrounding nations, Israel will not be confused in her singular allegiance to Yahweh or tempted to offer her worship to other gods. Keep in mind that Israel's sacred space did not necessarily look different from that of their neighbors. But who it housed was very different. Rather than being occupied by a statue covered in gold and silver, their sacred space was occupied by the all-powerful but invisible God. Rather than a god who was hungry and needed sacrifice to satisfy his cravings, the sacred space was occupied by a God who "owned the cattle on

> *a thousand hills" and valued obedience far more than sacrifice (Ps 50:10; 1 Sam 15:22). As a result, the means by which Yahweh was worshiped and the expectations he placed on his people were dramatically different than worship practices in Canaan as well.*[26]

How Does All of This Relate to the New Testament and to Us Here and Now?

The New Testament frequently uses creation language to describe the future after Christ's return. In Revelation 21:1, John writes, *"Then I saw a new heaven and a new earth, for the first heaven and the first earth had passed away."* In the end, God will not destroy the earth but will transform it. If we are rulers, as God originally intended for humanity, what does that mean for us? When Christ restores the earth upon His return, Christians will share in His rule. Revelation 19:16 declares that He is the *"King of kings."* Christ is the King, and Christians will be the kings.

We've explored the Old Testament through the lens of ancient culture, a perspective that was far different from what we find significant today. The ancient world had a different understanding of how the cosmos operated. God, however, met them where they were, taking the familiar and using it to reveal more about Himself. Moses wasn't primarily trying to teach Israel about the mechanics of creation. He wanted them to understand *why* God created the world.

Our reading of the creation story should help us grasp the immense value we have in God's eyes. We were created to be priests, working alongside Yahweh to bring order to the cosmos. This perspective sets the stage for what follows in Scripture. As in every story, there is a problem, and in the next chapter, we'll focus on that problem and its significance.

CHAPTER FOUR

How Far the Fall?

Yahweh has created a cosmos rich in abundance, providing everything for humanity and granting them the privilege of working alongside Him to bring order to creation. However, we now encounter the central problem in this unfolding narrative. The text does not specify how much time passed between the idyllic harmony of Adam and Eve's placement in the garden and the emergence of this crisis. Rather than a singular, isolated event, it is likely part of an ongoing pattern. In Genesis 3, we witness the transition from paradise to paradise lost—the fall of humanity, in which God's people, dwelling in God's place, reject God's rule.

The Serpent

This episode introduces a new character in the unfolding drama—a serpent. To understand its significance, we must first consider the nature of this creature. Studies indicate that nearly half of the population experiences some level of anxiety toward snakes, with approximately three percent meeting the criteria for a clinical phobia.[1]

In the Near Eastern cultures of the Bible, a walking serpent was a symbol of evil. Ancient audiences would have immediately recognized this imagery as representing something inherently dangerous. The serpent embodied deception, misdirection, and chaos.[2] Its description in Genesis is not meant to tell us what kind of creature it was in a biological sense, but rather to emphasize its role as a cunning and malevolent force.

Scripture does not explicitly explain the serpent's origins, but its identity becomes clear. The book of Revelation identifies it as Satan: *And the great dragon was thrown down, the serpent of old who is called the devil and Satan, who deceives the whole world; he was thrown down to the earth, and his angels were thrown down with him* (Rev. 12:9).

Elsewhere, he is also referred to as a dragon (Rev. 20:2) and Leviathan (Job 41).[3] But where did he come from? Peter offers insight: *For if God did not spare angels when they sinned, but cast them into hell and committed them to pits of darkness, reserved for judgment* (2 Pet. 2:4).

This passage suggests that Satan, like other fallen angels, was cast down as a consequence of rebellion. His presence in the garden signals the entrance of deception and disorder into God's perfect creation.

Is Satan merely the dark side to God's force, as in *Star Wars*? This is a misunderstanding we must avoid. The biblical narrative does not present two equal and opposing powers; rather, God reigns supreme, and Satan operates as a rebellious but ultimately subordinate being.

Because Genesis was written for a culture that thought in vivid imagery, we must consider the symbolic picture being painted. What kind of creature does Eve encounter? Why does she engage in conversation rather than flee if serpents were seen as evil?

The Hebrew word for "serpent" carries meanings beyond the literal—suggesting something both "shiny" and "enchanting."[4] This gives insight into why Eve was drawn into dialogue rather than recoiling in fear. Additionally, Genesis 3:1 describes the serpent as a*rum* or "crafty" or "cunning."[5] This is a term that plays on a Hebrew word closely related to "naked," used in 2:7 to describe the innocence of Adam and Eve.[6] This contrast highlights the serpent's shrewdness against humanity's initial purity.

It is crucial to recognize that this adversary has been at work for a long time. He is far too subtle to tempt someone outright to commit heinous acts like murder. Instead, he works through deception, leading people to hatred, which, as Jesus teaches, is murder in the heart.

The word "crafty" can also be translated as "smooth," implying that the serpent was a persuasive and deceptive speaker.[7] His words concealed his true intentions. Interestingly, "crafty" does not always carry a negative connotation. In the Book of Proverbs, the same Hebrew term is used positively, conveying the ideas of prudence and sensibility. For example, the NIV translates it in phrases such as:

- "A prudent man conceals dishonor" (Prov. 12:16).
- "A prudent man conceals knowledge" (Prov. 12:23).

- "Every prudent man acts with knowledge" (Prov. 13:16).
- "A prudent man sees evil and hides himself" (Prov. 22:3).

This contrast highlights how wisdom can be used for either good or deceit, depending on the intent behind it.

When God created Adam and Eve, He formed them as fully developed humans, yet emotionally, they were like children—innocent and untested. They needed to learn that true wisdom begins with the fear of the Lord. Instead of allowing the serpent to question her, Eve should have been the one questioning him.

The idea of a talking snake is difficult for many to comprehend or believe. However, it is important to recognize that the serpent is described this way to convey an image of danger and deception rather than to provide a biological classification.

When considering the nature of this creature, I align with Adam Clarke, the Methodist theologian of the late 18th and early 19th centuries. Clarke notes that while several Hebrew words are translated as "serpent," they offer little clarity in determining the most precise meaning. He highlights the linguistic connection between Hebrew and Arabic, where a similar root word, *chanas* or *khanasa*, carries meanings such as "to depart," "to withdraw," "to lie hidden," "to seduce," or "to slink away." From this root come the words *akhnas*, *khanasa*, and *khanoos*, all of which refer to an ape or a creature of the ape family. It is remarkable also from the same root comes *khanas*, a term used for the Devil—describing one who "draws off" or "seduces," emphasizing his role in leading people away from righteousness and obedience to God.[8]

Adam Clarke goes on to point out that with this linguistic insight in mind, we can now consider several key aspects of this mysterious creature.

1. He was superior to other animals in wisdom and understanding.

2. He originally walked upright, as implied by his punishment—"on your belly you will go"—which suggests a change in posture.

3. He possessed the ability to speak, as evidenced by his conversation with Eve.

4. He demonstrated reasoning skills, engaging in logical discourse and disputation with Eve.

5. These traits were likely common to him, as Eve showed no surprise at his ability to walk, talk, and reason. The way the text presents their interaction suggests that this was not their first conversation but part of an ongoing dialogue.

6. If this creature had never spoken before, its sudden ability to address Eve on such a profound subject would have undoubtedly startled her and made her more cautious. However, given her purity and innocence, she may have been incapable of experiencing fear or suspicion.

7. No known serpent has ever walked upright. The very word *serpent* is derived from the Latin *serpo*, meaning

> "to creep." If serpents had always moved in this manner, then being condemned to crawl on their bellies would not constitute a curse or punishment but merely a continuation of their natural state.[9]

It seems plausible that the creature described here was of the ape or orangutan kind, serving as the most suitable instrument for Satan's deceptive purposes. Satan operated through this creature, using it to carry out his scheme against humanity's life and soul. Hidden within it, he seduced our first parents and then withdrew—unseen by all except the all-seeing eye of God.

One doctor, known by Adam Clake, observed in the anatomy of the orangutan that it appears structurally designed for upright walking. However, these creatures exhibit a strong aversion to walking erect, requiring extensive discipline to be trained to do so.[10]

While our beliefs about the serpent's nature do not affect our salvation, this perspective offers a reasonable and plausible explanation. For those who struggle with parts of the Bible that seem too mythical, this interpretation provides a more credible answer to the question of the serpent's identity.

Regardless of how we envision the serpent's appearance, we can be certain of his purpose. As Jesus said, he came *"to steal, kill, and destroy"* (John 10:10).

The Snake's Tactics

Why did God allow the couple to be tempted? Can freedom exist without limitations? Adam and Eve were created as free moral agents, but their freedom had boundaries. Our freedom exists within God's prevenient grace; it is not absolute. For example, while I might wish I could fly like a bird, unless I board an airplane, that wish will never be realized. True freedom doesn't mean doing anything we want—it must have limits. Without such boundaries, we would descend into chaos and anarchy. Therefore, while temptation is not good in itself, it is necessary for the exercise of free will.

The couple was commanded not to eat from the "tree of the knowledge of good and evil." But what exactly was this tree? Leon Kass provides a helpful description, explaining that it represents "the autonomous knowledge of how to live, derived by human beings from their own experience of the visible world, and it is rooted in their surroundings."[11] Disobedience, in this context, means acting independently from God's definition of good and evil, making decisions based solely on our personal experience and what seems advantageous to us.

The Serpent's Deception

How does the serpent persuade Eve? He deceives her. As Paul writes in 1 Timothy 2:14, "*And Adam was not deceived, but the woman being deceived, fell into transgression.*" So, how does the serpent accomplish this? From the text, we can identify four key methods by which the devil deceives.

First, he creates doubt: "Did God really say that?" This question challenges the foundation of Eve's understanding and sets the stage for deception.

What is the difference between the decision-making of animals and humans? The serpent, though one of the beasts of the field, was clever and capable of speech. But how did he make decisions? Some scholars suggest that the Hebrew in Genesis 3:1 could be awkwardly interpreted as "Even if God said don't eat." The translation we read, "Has God said don't eat?" captures the intended sense, but the original language could also imply, "Even if God has said don't eat, so what?" This is the serpent's perspective.

As an animal is guided by its appetites, the serpent, embodying this animalistic nature, insinuates that Eve should follow her desires without concern for God's command. This resonates with the New Testament concept of the carnal nature. Webster defines "carnal" as "pertaining to or characterized by the flesh or the body, its passions, and appetites."[12] Animals are driven by instinct—they act based on desire, without regard for anything else. The serpent, acting in a similar manner, encourages Eve to do the same.

Eve, drawn by the allure of the tree, was tempted to follow her desires. The serpent told her to act on what felt right, implying that if it felt good, it couldn't possibly be wrong. Eve saw that the tree was as appealing as she had imagined. But the saying holds: *all that glitters is not gold.* Just because something looks good doesn't mean it is good (Proverbs 5:3-5). Eve judged based on appearances. This is like a toddler who keeps crying, "I want that!" His nanny repeatedly tells him no, but eventually, the mother, tired of the complaining, says, "Whatever it is, let him have it." The nanny, without further question, gives in to the child's demand, a bumble bee, leading to painful consequences.

Eve's Response

At first, Eve defends God's command. However, she adds to what God said, stating that God forbids them from even touching the fruit. But God never said this. In this moment, Eve becomes the first to engage in the practice of "building fences around the law."[13] This later evolved into the *Mishna*, which was a body of laws, customs, and usages that were developed after the exile and circulated in oral form. It became known as the oral law, considered just as authoritative as the written law.[14] This tradition would ultimately expand into 613 laws, making Eve the first to add to God's Word and setting a precedent for legalism.

The enemy, however, is not limited to one method of deception. He uses multiple tactics, and his next strategy is lying. In verse 4, he directly contradicts God, claiming that they would not die as God said. *"You won't really die,"* he asserts. This lie suggests that the consequences of their actions can be avoided.

In verse 5, the serpent distorts God's motives. He suggests that God is withholding something good from them: *"God knows that in the day you eat from it, your eyes will be opened, and you will be like God, knowing good and evil."* Interestingly, Adam and Eve already knew good and evil—they had experienced God's blessings and lived in abundance. God had already told them that eating from the tree was wrong, and they understood that. In Hebrew, the word "know" implies experiential knowledge rather than intellectual knowledge.[15] They had already tasted the goodness of God.

The serpent subtly portrays God as being hostile to humanity, suggesting that God is jealous and self-protective, unwilling to share His privileges with humans.[16] This distortion of God's character is the third tactic in the devil's scheme.

Finally, the serpent promises that eating the fruit will benefit Eve. When she looks at the fruit, she sees that it is good. Remember, when God created everything, He saw that it was good—everything was functioning according to His design, benefitting humanity. Now, however, Eve is evaluating things based on her own judgment rather than God's truth.

What is the opposite of doubt? Faith. And where has Eve placed her faith? In the serpent. In verses 2 and 3, Eve recalls that they were not to eat from the tree in the middle of the Garden. However, this tree—the one in the middle—is the Tree of Life, which they were permitted to eat from. Interestingly, God never forbids them from eating from the Tree of Life, and some believe they may have regularly eaten from it.

When the serpent redirects Eve's attention to the forbidden tree, she sees that the fruit is good. But just because something appears good doesn't make it legitimate. Some things may be lawful but not beneficial. If the fruit is good, why would God forbid them from eating it? The real rebellion here is Eve's desire to determine for herself what is right and wrong, rather than trusting God's definition. The essence of this rebellion is summed up in the attitude of, "We will do what we want to do, regardless of what You say." This is a mindset we see today in relativism, where people cry, "Don't try to force your morality on me," or "We can't legislate morality," claiming it as a form of freedom.

The Heart of Sin

At the core of sin lies selfishness and pride. Sin represents a reversal—what God has defined as wrong can suddenly seem right. It is characterized by a desire for independence from God. Wisdom, as a concept, is inherently good, and it is reasonable to assume that God did not intend to withhold it from humanity. However, true wisdom must be acquired through a process, typically learned from those who are wise.

The fall, therefore, is marked by the fact that Adam and Eve sought wisdom in an illegitimate way (Genesis 3:22).[17] This leads to the question: When did Eve sin? At what point did temptation turn into sin? The answer is that the moment Eve reached for the fruit, even before she ate it, she had already sinned.

The Consequences

I often tell my students, "You can do anything you want. What you cannot do is choose the consequences." Adam and Eve chose to believe the devil rather than God. In order for humanity to work alongside God in extending order—through the commands to "subdue" and "rule" (Gen 1:28)—wisdom is necessary. But this wisdom should be received as an endowment from God, not seized for personal use. Their failure to do so resulted in humanity's doom: death and a disordered world plagued by sin.

In contrast, Christ achieved the desired result that Adam and Eve failed to attain. Because of their sin, we are all doomed to die, having lost access to the Tree of Life. We are, therefore, subject to death because of sin. However, Christ succeeded where they failed, providing the remedy for both sin and death.[18]

Eve gives the fruit to Adam, and what had taken twenty verses to describe in Genesis 2 (5-25) takes just one verse (3:6) to unravel. The fall is summarized in four verbs: she saw, she took, she ate, and she gave.[19] It seems from the text that Adam wasn't far from Eve—he was with her. We read, *"She took from its fruit and ate, and she gave also to her husband with her, and he ate."* Why didn't Adam stop her? He knew better than to eat the fruit, so why did he do it? While Eve was deceived, Adam ate with his eyes wide open. His greater concern was about what Eve thought, rather than what God had said.

Further Effects

The instant Adam and Eve ate the fruit, they began to die. While their physical death didn't occur immediately, significant changes began right away. The first thing we see in verse 7 is, "Then the eyes of both of them were opened." Let's consider the Ancient Near Eastern (ANE) understanding of creation, described in the previous chapter, where the image is enlivened by the washing of the eyes. We can see that here, instead of being made alive, the couple begins to die and will eventually be banished.[20]

In verse 8, we read, *"They heard the sound of the LORD God walking in the garden in the cool of the day, and the man and his wife hid themselves from the presence of the LORD God among the trees of the garden."* They realized they were exposed and tried to cover themselves and hide. But why did they hide? What were they trying to conceal? We hide out of shame, which arises from the gap between who we are and who we believe we should be.[21] In this moment, Adam and Eve became self-conscious. As we often do, they began to care about whether they measured up to an idealized self-image, and they anxiously looked to others for validation of their worth.[22]

Thus, the first result of their sin is guilt and shame.

The Second Result: Evading Responsibility

In verse 9, we see a second result: God calls out to Adam, "*Where are you?*" Surely, the all-knowing God knows exactly where Adam is. After all, there is nowhere Adam can hide from God. So, God's question isn't about Adam's physical location. Instead, God is asking Adam to recognize the state of his relationship with Him. He is not where he's supposed to be. Something has drastically changed, and both God and Adam are aware of it.

In verses 12-13, both Adam and Eve attempt to avoid responsibility and shift the blame onto one another. Of the ten words Adam speaks, nine are self-justifying. Of the four words Eve speaks, three are self-justifying.[23] I once heard John Maxwell say, "When you blame, you b-lame." Jordan Peterson has a marvelous video on "Responsibility," and he says,

> *We know we are not all we could be, and we know we are not doing what we should do, and*

> *we are doing what we should not do. That should bother us. But we can take responsibility for our life and make it better than it is. We could blame how messed up we are in society, our parents, or how bad we have had it. We can be bitter, but that won't make life any better. We can wallow in our misery and suffering, but will that make us or the world any better? No. Or, we can take responsibility for our life and today determine to do something that will make it a little better.*[24]

When it comes to Adam and Eve's responsibility as priests of the Garden, that meant they were to guard it, and they neglected that duty and allowed the serpent in. They should have run him out of the Garden. Before this, they were intended to rule over all the creatures, and on this occasion, they obey one of the creatures.[25]

The Third Result of Sin: Concealing, Denying, and the Need for Confession

Sin causes us to conceal and deny rather than confess. Why do we do that? We are skilled at defending ourselves because, deep down, we know that God is our Judge. If you had to stand before Him in court, what would you do to prepare? You wouldn't try to defend yourself; you would want a powerful attorney. So, what if, when we sinned, we didn't have to defend our actions? The Bible tells us that Jesus is our Advocate—our

Lawyer before God. Because we have an Advocate, we don't need to defend ourselves. We are free to confess our sins and be forgiven. As 1 John 1:8-9 says, *"If we say that we have no sin, we are deceiving ourselves and the truth is not in us. If we confess our sins, He is faithful and righteous to forgive us our sins and to cleanse us from all unrighteousness."*

The Blame for the Fall

It's interesting that Eve ate the fruit first, yet Adam is blamed for the introduction of sin into the world. Paul writes in Romans 5:12, *"Therefore, just as through one man sin entered the world, and death through sin, and thus death spread to all men...."* Why is Adam blamed for the world's sin, even though Eve ate first? Because Adam was created first, and Eve was formed from his side. He was given the responsibility to protect and guide Eve, but instead, she led him into sin. This introduces another result of sin.

Disorder in the World

Adam was meant to work with God to bring order to the world. However, when the serpent entered—bringing chaos with him—the world became a place of disorder. This disorder is evident in the way we harm the environment, one another, and ourselves. Sin has disrupted the good order God designed for the world.

When Adam sinned, it wasn't just a personal failure—it created an environment of pollution. Just like a polluted stream affects everything downstream, Adam's sin polluted the environment, and we now live in a toxic world. Paul addresses this in Romans 5:13, *"Until the Law, sin was in the world, but sin is not imputed when there is no law."* This speaks to accountability.[26] Adam had only one law to obey, and he was accountable to God for that command. His failure to uphold that law resulted in the disorder and brokenness we now experience in creation.

A Darkened View of God

A final consequence of the fall is that it entrenched dark thoughts of God in our minds. Dane Ortlund poignantly said, "The fall also entrenched in our minds dark thoughts of God." He continues, "Perhaps Satan's greatest victory in your life is… the dark thoughts of God's heart that… keep you cool toward Him…."[27] When we know we have done wrong, our natural inclination is to avoid the one we have wronged. However, it's important to recognize that the very reason Jesus came and died was to forgive us.

Imagine a doctor who travels thousands of miles, bringing all the necessary medicine and technology to heal sick people in a remote area. Yet, instead of allowing the doctor to treat their illness, the people hide. Jesus, too, came from His glorious home to heal our sin-sickness. Will we hide from Him or run to Him for healing?

The Lie of the Serpent

It's also interesting to note that when the couple eats the fruit, their eyes are opened, but instead of becoming like God, as the serpent promised, they discover something entirely different. They become acutely aware of their nakedness and their shame, which starkly contrasts with the serpent's promise. Their understanding is now clouded—not illuminated to be like God—but darkened by sin. This illustrates how sin distorts God's truth, making us perceive the world in ways that lead us further from Him.

The Loss of Relationship and Dominion

When we assess the damage caused by the couple's rebellion, we see it in the loss of both their relationship with God and their dominion over creation. Dominion here reflects the concept of a kingdom—authority, and responsibility entrusted to them. However, the loss of relationship with God carries far greater consequences. It's important to recognize that the effects of the fall are descriptive, not prescriptive. God is not actively causing the consequences; rather, they are the natural results of the man's and woman's choices.

In understanding the loss of dominion and relationship, we don't need further details to grasp the severity of the consequences. In military terms, we might refer to this as "collateral damage"—unintended but inevitable harm that extends beyond the target. The breakdown of the relationship with God creates a ripple effect that permeates all of creation.

God had said they would die, and indeed, they did. But what is death? Death is the separation of the body from the soul. It began with the separation in their relationship with

God, the ultimate source of life. This death was more than just estrangement; it was a total break. Before the fall, Adam enjoyed a perfect harmony in his work with God, a seamless connection where he and God were as one. Now, that union was shattered.

To illustrate this, I have an old pair of work gloves that fit perfectly. When I wear them, I can do any tough job, as they protect my hands while allowing my fingers to manipulate and work. In a similar way, Adam had been so united with God that he functioned effortlessly, as though God were the hand and Adam the glove. The fall severed this connection. The moment Adam and Eve separated from God, they also detached themselves from the source of blessing. Instead, by their actions, they chose to align themselves with the devil.

The Ripple Effect of Separation

The separation caused by sin doesn't stop with the individual's relationship with God. In verse 15, God declares that there will be ongoing conflict between the offspring of the woman and the serpent's offspring. With the loss of their intimate connection with God, humanity is now caught in a constant struggle between those who follow God and those who align themselves with evil. This conflict will be evident soon, beginning in Chapter 4.

Further, in verse 16, God reveals that there will be a perpetual power struggle between men and women. The woman will desire to dominate the man, and the man will seek to dominate the woman. This is not how it was meant to be. In Ephesians 5:22-25, the Apostle Paul offers a clearer vision of the relationship between husband and wife:

> *"Wives, be subject to your own husbands, as to the Lord. For the husband is the head of the wife, as Christ also is the head of the church, He Himself being the Savior of the body. But as the church is subject to Christ, so also the wives ought to be to their husbands in everything. Husbands, love your wives, just as Christ also loved the church and gave Himself up for her."*

Sin has introduced a dysfunction into the relationship between men and women. The perfect partnership that was originally designed by God has been marred. Jesus clarified that when something goes wrong in our relationship with God, it inevitably affects our relationships with one another. We see this in the way Adam and Eve hide not only from God but from each other. There is a loss of intimacy, a separation that now exists between them.

Why, then, are we often not open or vulnerable with others? Why do we hide our fears and struggles? The answer lies in a lack of trust. We fear that what we share may be used against us. We wonder if we will be rejected or, worse, if our vulnerabilities will be exposed and used to shame us. This distrust in others is a consequence of the brokenness introduced by sin, and it continues to disrupt our relationships.

The Internal Separation and the Impact on Creation

In addition to the relational separation between humanity and God, there is a more subtle form of alienation: we also separate from ourselves. We begin to hide our own true needs and desires. People often seek psychological counseling in hopes of uncovering the dysfunctions within themselves—an attempt to reconcile with who they truly are. The term "dysfunctional family" is commonly used, but the truth is, since the fall, every family has been dysfunctional in some way, though the degree of dysfunction varies.

This internal disconnection reflects the larger impact of sin on all of creation. The harmony between humanity and the earth is broken. In verse 17, God tells Adam that now the ground will produce thorns and thistles. Recall the connection between **Adamah** (the ground) and **Adam**, and how this bond has been fractured by sin. Where there was once a cooperative relationship between humanity and the earth, there will now be a struggle. The earth no longer yields its bounty without toil.

Similarly, God tells Eve that childbirth will be painful. The place of greatest joy for a woman—bringing new life into the world—will now be marred by suffering. The fall introduced pain and difficulty into what should have been moments of fulfillment and purpose. The fulfillment Adam found in his work will now be tainted by hardship and sweat, and the joy Eve found in family life will now be accompanied by the pain of childbirth.

God's Grace in the Midst of Judgment

We must not overlook a key detail: animals had to die immediately to provide clothing for Adam and Eve. While the fall brought immediate consequences, including spiritual death and the loss of access to the Tree of Life, God's provision of clothing was an act of grace. This moment foreshadows the ultimate sacrifice that would be required to restore humanity—life would come through death, a theme that echoes throughout Scripture.

As we mentioned earlier, Adam and Eve had access to the Tree of Life, and it is likely that they had eaten from it. However, with their expulsion from the Garden, they could no longer partake of it, making death inevitable. In this separation from God, who is the source of life, humanity lost not only communion with the Creator but also the very purpose of their existence: to work alongside God in bringing order and stewardship to the world.[28]

Despite their rebellion, God's compassion is evident in how He clothed them. This act was not just a provision for their immediate need—it was a tangible expression of His continued care and love for His creation. Even in the face of their sin, God was working toward redemption. The rest of the Bible is a story of how God seeks to restore both the relationship with humanity and the purpose for which we were originally created.

The expulsion from Eden is emphasized in several important ways. First, there is a repeated description of Yahweh's action in expelling Adam (vv. 23–24), which intensifies from simply being "sent out" to "driven out." This stronger language underscores the severity of the consequence. Once driven out, access to Eden is barred with a double barrier: the cherubim, fierce angelic guardians, and the flaming, whirling sword. This act of exclusion is not merely a separation but a dramatic and sacred one, ensuring no easy return to Eden.

This raises the profound question: How can humanity return to what was once considered sacred space? The psalmist in Psalm 24:3 asks, *"Who may ascend into the hill of the LORD?"* This question sets the tone for the "Gate Liturgy," a ritual performed by the Hebrew people when they approached the tabernacle or temple. The priest guarding the precincts would ask, *"Who shall ascend the mountain of Yahweh? Who shall stand in His holy place?"* The people would respond, *"He who has clean hands and a pure heart, who has not lifted up his soul to falsehood and has not sworn deceitfully."* This liturgy highlighted the necessary purity and holiness for entering God's presence.[29]

Moreover, it is significant that the direction they traveled was eastward—away from Eden and away from the sacred Mountain of God. This eastward movement will carry symbolic weight throughout the rest of Scripture, indicating a continual journey further from God's intended presence and order.

Where Are We?

Where does this leave us today? We currently live in a world of mixed realities—order, disorder, and non-order. When God initially brought order to creation, there were still elements of non-order. For example, there was the sea, even though its boundaries had been established, and there was still darkness. Outside the Garden, there was an environment even less ordered than inside it. The full resolution of this non-order will only be realized in the new creation.

In Revelation 21, we are given a vision of this future: "*There will be no longer any sea*" (Rev 21:1), *no pain or death* (Rev 21:4), and *no darkness* (Rev 21:23-25). The new creation will be characterized by an unparalleled level of order, a perfection that has never before existed.

Before the fall, the world was a combination of order and non-order, with God's ongoing strategy to bring more order.[30] This mission will continue, but now it will be accomplished through Jesus Christ—at the great cost of His blood being shed upon the cross. His work, the ultimate restoration, will bring final order to the world, where every trace of disorder and non-order will be removed.

In Genesis 3:14, we observe that God cursed the serpent, but He did not curse Adam directly. However, by aligning himself with the cursed one, Adam became complicit in the curse. Adam and Eve desired a world without God, and tragically, that is what they got. Yet, despite the consequences of their rebellion, God sets out to redeem humanity from their predicament.

When Adam and Eve chose to take the "knowledge of good and evil" (Genesis 2:17) for themselves, they essentially sought to be like God. As a result, they inherited the responsibility to establish and sustain order—something they were not equipped to do on their own. In the end, they were sent out into a chaotic world, tasked with bringing order to it, a mission they attempted but failed at miserably.

Their initial role had been to guard the Garden of Eden, but now, instead of protecting it, an angel with a flaming sword was placed at the gate to prevent their re-entry. The Garden, once a place of harmony, was now closed off, reflecting the greater separation from God that their disobedience had caused.

Before we move to Genesis 4, it's worth noting an interesting development in the relationship between Adam and Eve. In Genesis 2, when Adam first encounters Eve, he names her "woman." However, in Genesis 3:20, Adam gives her the name "Eve" because she is the "mother of all living." This is significant because, at that point, Eve had not yet given birth to any children. Yet, after the fall, when Eve conceives and gives birth to Cain, Adam recognizes her newfound role as the giver of life. This marks a pivotal shift in how Adam perceives Eve and her place in the world.

From this moment onward, the concept of life-giving becomes central, and the significance of women in bearing and nurturing life is highlighted. Additionally, it foreshadows how, from here on out, human significance will often be measured through actions such as heroic deeds, accomplishments, and even battles. Eve's role as the "mother of all living" sets the stage for understanding the weight of human identity in terms of creation, survival, and legacy.[31]

CHAPTER FIVE
No Order to Order

As we arrive at Genesis 4, we witness the spread of sin. It is important to understand that sin is not merely a bad action—it is a form of pollution. Just as physical pollution affects everyone in its vicinity, so too does spiritual pollution. After Adam and Eve are expelled from the Garden of Eden, their sinful state prevents them from meeting with God face to face as they once did. Many scholars believe that the entrance to the Garden became a sacred meeting place where Adam, Eve, and their descendants would worship God and bring their sacrifices.[1] It is here that we are introduced to the story of their two sons, Cain and Abel.

From Rebellion to Fratricide to Brutality

Sin did not remain an isolated event; it escalated. What began as rebellion in the Garden now progresses to fratricide—the killing of a brother. The turning point in this story revolves around an offering to God. Both Cain and Abel bring their gifts, yet, intriguingly, God rejects Cain's offering. Why?

Imagine two children drawing pictures for their father. One child takes time and care, filling the page with detailed birds, trees, flowers, and clouds. When the father sees the drawing, he praises the child and proudly displays it on the refrigerator. Seeing this, the other child hurriedly sketches a few stick figures and presents it. How should the father respond? Should he offer the same praise simply to be fair? That is how most of us would react.

God does not operate this way. His response to Cain is not about comparing his offering to Abel's—it is about evaluating Cain's gift in light of what he was capable of giving. Interestingly, Cain was the first to bring an offering, yet the issue was not the type of gift or who gave first, but its quality. Abel, a shepherd, gave the best of his flock, while Cain, a farmer, merely offered some of his produce rather than his finest yield. The difference was not in what they brought, but in how they brought it—Abel gave his best, while Cain did not.

Cain perceived Abel's offering as an attempt to outdo him.[2] But does God actually need offerings? As the Creator of the universe, the Almighty, what could anyone possibly give to Him? This leads us to a deeper question about the nature of their offerings. Why did Cain and Abel present gifts to God in the first place?

Why do we give gifts to others? Sometimes, we give out of gratitude; other times, we give as a form of insurance. Consider how someone might give a gift to their boss—perhaps as a token of appreciation for a job they are grateful to have, or perhaps as a way to secure continued employment. Abel's offering was an expression of gratitude, while Cain's was given to stay in God's favor. The true value of a gift, however, is not measured in its material worth but in the heart behind it.

A well-known story illustrates this point. An African boy once presented a missionary with a beautifully colored shell. Knowing such shells were not found inland, the missionary asked where he had found it. The boy replied, "From the ocean shore." He had walked miles to retrieve it. The missionary, astonished, remarked, "But that is a very long way off." The boy smiled and said, "The distance traveled is part of the gift." The true gift was not the shell itself but the effort and devotion behind it.

Was this one incident the sole reason Cain killed Abel? Consider Cain's position—he was the firstborn, the first human child ever born. Then came Abel, threatening his favored status. Cain now had to compete for his parents' attention and affection. While brothers may unite when facing an external threat, they are often rivals in times of peace. When God rejected his sacrifice, Cain likely perceived it as unfair. One writer notes, "This is the first instance of perceived injustice. Cain couldn't direct his anger at God, so he turned it against his brother."[3]

In the narrative, Moses repeats the word *brother* seven times. Why emphasize what is already obvious? This repetition underscores the importance of family loyalty—a theme woven throughout Scripture. We see it again in the story of Joseph and his brothers.[4] When Yahweh confronts Cain about Abel's whereabouts, Cain responds defiantly, *"Am I my brother's keeper?"* (Gen. 4:9). This response is telling. As the firstborn, he bore responsibility for his younger brother.[5] The same principle is later highlighted in the story of Joseph (Gen. 37:8, 19–20), where sibling rivalry and betrayal stand in stark contrast to the expectation of kinship loyalty. This tension—between loyalty and betrayal—becomes a recurring theme throughout Israel's history.[6]

In verse 12, God tells Cain that he will become a wanderer. At first, this might not sound like a severe punishment, but consider Cain's identity—he was a farmer. His life revolved around working the soil, planting, and harvesting. Now, that life was over. No longer would he cultivate the land; instead, he would be doomed to endless wandering.

This also meant that Cain would live as a desert nomad. In the ancient world, the desert, much like the chaotic waters in Genesis 1, was seen as a refuge for the disgraced, a dwelling place for outlaws. It was a hostile land, home to demons and wild beasts.[7] The text tells us that Cain went to the land of *Nod*, a name that fittingly means "wandering."[8]

Much debate has surrounded the mark of Cain mentioned in verse 15. This mark was not a *stigma* of condemnation but rather a sign of belonging to a group in which blood vengeance was ruthlessly enforced.[9] As Dr. Yigal Bloch describes, blood vengeance...

> *Blood vengeance is also found in northern Mesopotamia. The Middle Assyrian Laws, from the city of Assur in the 12th century B.C.E., note that a man has the right to avenge a murdered*

relative by killing the killer, or he can just take payment, including one of the killer's children if nothing else is available:

[If either] a man or a woman enters [another man's] house and kills [either a man] or a woman, [they shall hand over] the manslayers [to the head of the household]: if he so chooses, he shall kill them, or if he chooses to come to an accommodation, he shall take [their property]; and if there is [nothing of value to give from the house] of the manslayers, either a son [or a daughter . . .]

Blood vengeance is a form of justice in which the family or clan of the deceased has the right to punish the assailant. Such behavior likely originated in pre-state societies in which clans needed to maintain an equilibrium of power in which injury to one family was compensated by a comparable injury to the offending group. But such responses continued long after the emergence of states— they still exist in some societies nowadays—when the local clans are unwilling to submit to the central authority in this regard. This seems to be the case for biblical society.

In the period that the Pentateuch was composed, clearly, the leaders needed to deal with the clans,

> *who still felt that they had the right to take revenge on whoever killed their relative. Thus, the laws here represent a compromise between the idealized Israelite society, with judgments made by an objective third-party, and clannish justice, in which the blood avenger hunts down the killer and takes revenge. Part of this compromise is the building of refuge cities for the manslayer, which, in addition to protecting his life, punishes unintentional killers by forcing them to live in exile for an extended period, thus calming the tempers of the offended clan. If the person leaves early, it is assumed that society will not be able to offer protection, and the blood avenger will act.*[10]

In verses 16–17, we read that Cain built a city—an act that implies the presence of other people beyond Adam, Eve, and their two sons. Cities, by their very nature, exist to accommodate large groups. This suggests that God may have created more than just a single couple. Cain names the city after his son, a reflection of humanity's enduring quest for glory and immortality. In the Ancient Near East, as in many other cultures, a person's name was preserved through monumental achievements—whether through building projects, military victories, or descendants.[11]

Later, in verses 19–24, we encounter Lamech, who boasts to his wives about killing a man for merely wounding him. His arrogance and violence mark a disturbing escalation of sin—one that moves beyond Cain's act of fratricide to unrestrained brutality. What does this reveal about sin? One of its consequences is its own multiplication. Sin begets more sin, deepening its hold on humanity.

The Passing of the Blessing

In Genesis 4:25, after Abel's death, Adam and Eve have another son, Seth. His lineage, beginning with Enosh in Genesis 5:6, eventually leads to Noah, who will serve as a new Adam. Genesis 5 provides the genealogy of Adam, which some have mistakenly viewed as a third creation story. However, it is not another account of creation but rather the unfolding of the human story.

Genealogies play a crucial role throughout the Bible. They often serve as either the conclusion of one narrative or the introduction to another, ensuring that Scripture is not merely a collection of isolated stories but a continuous historical account. Some scholars have even referred to Genesis as the *Book of Generations*, a title found in Genesis 5:1. This first genealogy is particularly significant because it traces the lineage from Seth to Noah, emphasizing the continuation of the blessing. A key function of genealogies in biblical history is to reveal God's divine purpose, showing how history moves toward a specific goal.[12]

A striking contrast appears between Genesis 5:1 and 5:3. While Adam was created in the image of God, Seth is described as being in the image of Adam. Humanity still bears the image of God, but that image has been marred by sin. Additionally, as we read through Adam's genealogy, we notice a significant omission—Cain is not included. This exclusion highlights the conflict between two seeds, first mentioned in Genesis 3:15, the evil line of Cain and the godly line of Seth. This struggle continues throughout Scripture until the New Testament, where the seed of the woman—Jesus—ultimately crushes the head of the serpent, fulfilling God's promise.

One figure stands out in Genesis 5: Enoch, a descendant of Seth. He is distinct from Enosh and is remembered for his unique relationship with God. I heard it suggested that Yahweh and Enoch would take long walks together. One day, Yahweh is said to have told him, "Enoch, we're closer to My house than yours. Why don't you just come home with Me?" Unlike the others listed in this genealogy, Enoch does not die in the traditional sense; instead, he is taken by God (Genesis 5:23–24).

The genealogy of Genesis 5 highlights a fundamental truth—death reigns. Adam lived 930 years, and he died, fulfilling the prophecy that he would surely die.[13] Many of these figures lived extraordinarily long lives—Methuselah, for example, reached 969 years. Yet one reality remains constant: they all die. This genealogy underscores the mortality introduced by sin, a theme that echoes throughout Scripture.

A Second Adam

When we arrive at the story of Noah, we encounter the first person with no direct contact with Adam.[14] In Genesis 6:3, we also see a dramatic reduction in the human lifespan, now limited to 120 years.

Genesis 6 contains some of the most mysterious and troubling passages in the Old Testament. One particularly perplexing statement describes how the "sons of God" saw that the "daughters of men" were beautiful, took them as wives, and bore children who were unlike any others—different, as were their fathers, the *sons of God.* The identity of these figures has been the subject of much speculation, and I will outline some of the most widely considered possibilities.

In verse 4, we encounter the *Nephilim*. The Hebrew root of *Nephilim* suggests meanings such as *to fall, to be cast down*, or even *to perish.*[15] Martin Luther described the Nephilim as men of violence—tyrants who wielded great power.[16] For lack of a better description, the Nephilim appear to have been a distinct race, different from anything else in creation, and their uniqueness was marked by evil.

It is as though the Nephilim were mutations or aberrations, possessing great strength and power. They embodied a fusion of the worst aspects of the spiritual and physical worlds. Their size, intelligence, and strength may have made them the subjects of ancient pagan myths—legends of mighty warriors and rulers with seemingly superhuman qualities. Some have speculated that the Nephilim were the same giants later found in the Promised Land and that even Goliath may have been one of their descendants.

Lawson Stone understands it from an ANE perspective that is more credible. He says,

> *Seizing on the apparent connection between the term Nephilim and the Hebrew verb meaning*

> *"to fall," some immediately make a tie to "the fall" and think of these "fallen ones" as fallen angels. Indeed, when the Pharaohs of Egypt spoke of violently rebellious warlords in Canaan, they often called them "wretched fallen ones." On the other hand, that link to the verb meaning "to fall" might be weak as well. Another cognate language features the same word meaning, "To destroy, to tear down," so our Nephilim might well be "Destoyers" or the like. Since extreme violence figures into the reason for the flood in the Bible, Genesis 6:1-4, by providing a kind of genealogy for the abuse of power, provides a great prologue to the story.*[17]

As we approach the story of the flood, it is important to recognize that the biblical writer is not primarily concerned with proving the historical reality of the event. Instead, the focus is on interpreting its meaning. What was God doing? Why did Yahweh send the flood?

The flood narrative invites us to consider the moral and theological implications rather than simply its historical significance. While discussions of the flood's historicity persist, the biblical account emphasizes divine judgment, human corruption, and the possibility of renewal.

On a lighter note, Bill Cosby's comedic rendition of *Noah and the Flood*, available on YouTube, provides a humorous take on the story. Though not theologically precise, it is undeniably entertaining and offers a different perspective on how people engage with this well-known biblical event.

Other Flood Stories

When comparing the biblical flood narrative with those of the Ancient Near East (ANE), one of the most striking differences is how the divine realm is portrayed—what the gods are like and how they govern the cosmos.

In the Bible, Yahweh alone decrees the flood, warns Noah to preserve humanity, brings the waters, causes them to recede, receives Noah's sacrifice, and establishes a covenant with creation. His actions are purposeful, and his covenant ensures the ongoing stability of the world.

In contrast, Mesopotamian flood myths depict a pantheon of gods with conflicting interests. In the *Epic of Gilgamesh*, for example, Enlil orders the flood to destroy humanity, but Ea (Enki) opposes the plan. Recognizing that the gods rely on human labor for sustenance, Ea secretly warns his devotee, Utnapishti (the devotee), undermining Enlil's decree.[18] The other gods, having initially supported the destruction, panic when the flood begins, realizing too late that wiping out humanity also eliminates their food supply. Starved and desperate, they swarm around the post-flood sacrifice like flies.

This fundamental difference in worldview is rooted in what scholars call the "Great Symbiosis."[19] In Mesopotamian belief, the gods created humans not for relationship but out of necessity—they were weary of laboring to provide for themselves. Humans were tasked with growing food, building temples, and offering sacrifices to sustain the gods. This dependence created a codependent relationship: the gods needed humans for survival, and in return, they protected them. If there is no rain, crops cannot grow, and the gods cannot be fed. They needed to protect them because if they were being threatened by invaders who stole their food or burned their crops, the gods could not be cared for. Providing for the gods was the principal feature of their religious practice. Offense is failure to meet the needs of the gods. The flood in Mesopotamian mythology was not a moral judgment but a practical miscalculation. The gods regretted nearly destroying humanity, not because of any inherent value in people but because they needed them to survive.

The biblical account, however, presents a radically different view of the divine. Yahweh does not need humanity for sustenance. Instead, he creates people for relationships, with the intention of dwelling among them. His grief over human corruption is not a reflection of divine weakness or lack of foresight but of sorrow over broken communion.

God's Attitude Toward Mankind

By Genesis 6, sin has escalated, and violence has spread throughout humanity. Genesis 6:6 reveals a profound insight into God's emotions: *"The LORD was sorry that He had made man on the earth, and He was grieved in His heart."* The Hebrew word for "grieved," עָצַב (*'āṣab*)[20] conveys deep sorrow, the same word used to describe intense pain. It is rare for a biblical writer to provide such a glimpse into God's inner thoughts and feelings.

Genesis 6:12 emphasizes the extent of human corruption: *"The earth was filled with violence."* Murder had become rampant, signaling the depth of moral decay. This level of wickedness made divine intervention necessary—not just as an act of judgment but as a means of restoration. The situation can be likened to a rabid dog: once infected, the disease is irreversible, and the only humane solution is to put the animal down to prevent further suffering and harm.

Tracing the narrative structure of Genesis, we see a recurring pattern:

- Genesis 1:2 – The world begins in chaos, without form or order.
- Creation – God brings order to this chaos.
- Genesis 3 – Sin enters, disrupting God's order and introducing disorder.
- The Flood – God resets creation by allowing the chaotic waters to reclaim the world, washing away disorder before reestablishing order through Noah.

The flood serves as a cosmic "reset button." Noah's name means *"rest" "נֹחַ , from the root נוח (nûaḥ), meaning "rest" or "comfort"*[21] —not in the sense of relaxation, but in the sense of restored order. This aligns with Jesus' words in Matthew 11:28: *"Come to Me, all you who are weary and heavy-laden, and I will give you rest."* Here, *rest* signifies the peace and stability that come from divine order.

The Waters of the Flood

Where did all the water come from? The biblical imagery of the cosmos presents the universe as originally a vast, dark, watery abyss. In Genesis 1:6-8, God creates an "expanse" (often translated as "firmament") that separates the "waters above" from the "waters below." This forms a protective biosphere—a fragile but ordered space where life can flourish.

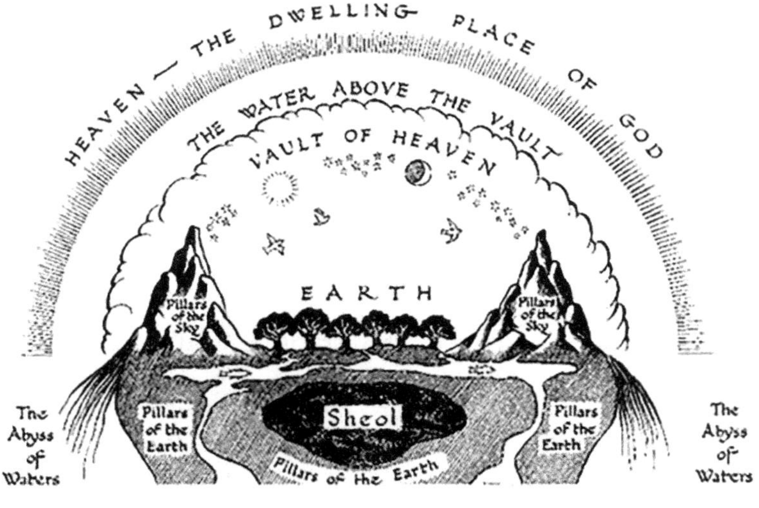

Fig. 5 Flood cosmology: (*Rayburn and Fry, 2000*)

During the flood, Genesis describes the *"windows of heaven"* opening and the *"fountains of the deep"* breaking apart. This suggests that the carefully ordered world—the "bubble" of creation—was ruptured, allowing the chaotic waters above and below to merge once again, effectively *uncreating* the world.[22]

The flood lasted **forty** days and nights. The number **seven** in the Bible signifies completion, while **forty** consistently represents a period of **testing and transformation**—seen in Moses' time on Mount Sinai, Israel's forty years in the wilderness, and Jesus' forty days of fasting in the desert. The flood, therefore, was not just a punishment but a period of divine refinement, leading to a new beginning.

The Noahic Covenant

Why did God choose Noah? First, Noah was part of the line of the blessing. His selection is significant because he possessed the attributes that would qualify him to stand before the presence of Yahweh. We are told in Genesis 6:9 that Noah was a *righteous* man, *blameless* in his generation. These qualities mirror the necessary prerequisites for ascending the mountain of God, as seen in earlier biblical narratives. In contrast to the pervasive corruption described in the world, Noah demonstrated the discernment to recognize the difference between true good and evil. Many scholars suggest that this is where the concept of natural law emerges—the understanding of moral order beyond mere human opinion.

The word *corrupt* in Genesis 6:12, which is used to describe humanity's state, is the same word used in Genesis 6:13 when Yahweh declares His intention to *destroy* the earth. This subtle wordplay reveals that the moral decay of humanity directly leads to God's decision to intervene with judgment. Noah's righteousness is the basis upon which his family is spared from the impending floodwaters of destruction.

Skipping to Genesis 9, we encounter the first covenant between God and humanity. The Hebrew word *berith* (covenant) means "to bind together," signifying a binding relationship.[23] Every covenant has three key elements: a promise, a sign, and requirements. In this covenant, God promises never to destroy the earth again with a flood. The sign of this promise is the rainbow, a symbol of peace. Interestingly, the rainbow is depicted as a weapon of war—a bow. But God's bow is aimed upward, not downward, at the earth. It signifies that God has hung up His weapon, signaling peace rather than war.

The requirements of this covenant are twofold:

1. The prohibition of consuming blood, as blood represents life itself.

2. The establishment of social order, including the prohibition of murder, which was to be punished by death. This is an important moment, as there is no provision for justifiable or accidental killing—every murder, whether intentional or unintentional, required the death of the murderer. This harsh requirement underscores the sanctity of human life, as we are made in the image of God. Justice, in this case, demands a fitting consequence—capital punishment. The aim is not vengeance but to honor the image of God in humanity. This principle highlights the gravity of sin and the seriousness of moral order.[24]

Historically, public executions in the 19th century often involved the entire community witnessing the event, a reminder of the communal recognition of the gravity of sin and punishment. The terrible nature of capital punishment reflects the terrible nature of sin itself.[25]

We need to view murder as an attack, not just on another human, but an attack on God. Genesis 1:26-27 and 2:5-3:24 Yahweh is portrayed as the father of humanity. Thus, because murder was understood as an attack on one's entire family, this would include God.[26]

In Genesis 9:7, we see God commanding Noah and his descendants, *"Be fruitful and multiply."* These words echo the command given to Adam in Genesis 1:28, but there are key differences. First, the presence of Yahweh is not explicitly stated here. Second, the blessing given to Noah does not include dominion over creation as it did for Adam. Instead, the emphasis is on the maintenance of social order.

Noah's Drunkenness and Ham's Transgression (Genesis 9:20-25)

In Genesis 9:20-25, we read about Noah's drunkenness and Ham's actions, which result in a curse upon Ham's son, Canaan. The phrase *"Ham, the father of Canaan, saw the nakedness of his father"* has sparked significant debate. This is widely regarded as a euphemism, a figure of speech in which something is said in a way that avoids a more direct or explicit description. In this case, there are several interpretations of what *"saw the nakedness of his father"* actually means:

1. Ham had sexual relations with Noah while he slept. Some suggest that this is the most direct reading, with

the phrase referring to an incestuous act between Ham and Noah.

2. Ham had sexual relations with Noah's wife. This interpretation holds that Ham's offense was not directly with Noah but with Noah's wife, possibly as an attempt to take advantage of Noah's vulnerability while he was drunk.

3. Ham disgraced Noah in some way. This interpretation suggests that Ham's actions were more about disrespecting his father—"unfathering" him, as some put it. By seeing his father's nakedness, he undermined Noah's authority and dignity in a way that shamed him.

4. Ham shamed his father in a broader, familial sense. A more common interpretation is that Ham shamed Noah through a lack of familial loyalty. The phrase "He kills his father as a father" from a Jewish writer might suggest that Ham, by failing to honor Noah in his vulnerability, dishonored the family structure as a whole.

5. The ambiguity of the phrase leaves room for these possibili-ties, but all interpretations center around the idea that Ham's action was deeply disrespectful. Noah's shame was not just personal—it carried implications for the family and the future generations.[27]

The Cursing of Canaan

It is striking that Noah curses Canaan, Ham's son, instead of Ham himself. This may be more than a simple act of paternal anger—it is often seen as a prophetic judgment. Noah's curse upon Canaan can be understood as a reflection of what kind of descendant Ham would raise. If Ham, as a father, demonstrated a lack of respect and loyalty, it is logical to think that his son would also embody these same traits. This pattern of generational sin appears throughout Scripture.

The curse on Canaan has prophetic overtones, especially in relation to the Canaanites, who would later be a constant threat to Israel. In Deuteronomy 7:1-3, God commands Israel to destroy the Canaanites, as they embody the corruption and disloyalty reflected in Ham's actions. The Canaanites, who fail to honor familial structures and covenantal relationships, represent a lasting challenge to Israel's identity and purity.

However, the curse is *not prescriptive*, in the sense that it doesn't necessarily dictate how future generations should behave. Rather, it is a *descriptive* judgment, illustrating the consequences of Ham's actions. It is a reminder that sin often affects not just the individual but also those who come after them.

Interestingly, Moab (from Lot, Abraham's nephew) is another example of familial connections in Scripture. In Deuteronomy 2:9, God tells Moses not to engage in battle with the Moabites because they are *family*—descendants of Lot, who is Abraham's nephew. This distinction shows how different familial dynamics play out in God's covenantal plan. While Canaan's descendants are to be destroyed because of their disloyalty and corruption, the Moabites, though not part of the covenant, are treated with a different regard due to their closer familial ties.

The Line of Shem, Japheth, and the Blessing

Shem is the ancestor of Abram (Abraham) and, by extension, the nation of Israel. Shem's descendants are often associated with those who walk in God's blessing and covenant. This is a key reason why God chooses Abram from the line of Shem—Abram's faith and obedience to God are part of God's unfolding plan of redemption through Shem's line.

Japheth, on the other hand, is traditionally seen as the ancestor of the Greeks and Europeans. Japheth's descendants are often linked with those who expand outward, colonizing new territories. While not part of the covenantal blessing in the same way as Shem, Japheth's line plays a role in the broader spread of humanity and cultures after the flood.

In Genesis 10:9, we encounter Nimrod, who is described as *"a mighty hunter before the LORD."* However, this could be translated as *"in the sight of the LORD," "opposite the LORD," "facing the LORD,"* or *"facing up to the LORD."*[28] This latter translation seems appropriate to describe Nimrod as an aggressive person. This runs counter to what God has intended mankind to be like in ruling the earth on His behalf. God originally intended man to rule the earth in peace, but Nimrod established a kingdom through aggression.[29]

The Spread of Nations

In Genesis 10:32, we find the answer to the question of how we got so many nations. Chapter eleven introduces us to the Tower of Babel. John Walton says,

> *The Tower of Babel represented the definitive formulation of a brand of paganism that pervaded the ancient Near East in which mythologized deity was portrayed as having all the foibles of humanity. In so doing, humanity remade deity in its own image. The perception of God that swept the ancient world was incapable of providing a sound basis for a relationship with the one true God. The result was the need for God to vouchsafe an accurate revelation of himself.*[30]

There are several explanations concerning the Tower of Babel. Many people believe the people were trying to reach God. However, if we understand a bit about the Ancient Near Eastern culture of the time, we learn that people built towers called ziggurats. These were sacred spaces, not for human use, but designed for the gods to descend upon. The people were building one of these towers. The actual name of the city is "Babylon," which means "gate of God," reflecting the belief that the ziggurat served as a gateway to heaven. However, the Hebrew word for Babylon, "Babel," is a pun meaning "nonsense" or "confusion," which reflects God's judgment.[31]

In Ancient Near Eastern thought, people believed the gods created humans as slave labor to serve them. In return, the gods would provide for them. Next to these ziggurats, temples were built for the gods to dwell in, where people could carry out their rituals. While this may seem reasonable, the people did not seek to worship God for His glory but for their own gain. As 11:4 says, *"Come, let us build for ourselves a city, and a tower whose top will reach into heaven, and let us make for ourselves a name..."* What were they trying to achieve? I am inclined to believe they were trying to do two things.

1. They wanted to manipulate God. They believed that if they built such an impressive structure, they would create a reputation for themselves, making them unassailable by others.

2. They wanted to return to sacred space. When Adam and Eve were cast out of the Garden, they lost access to the sacred space where God dwelt. The tower was an attempt to restore that closeness, as if bringing God down to be with them once again. God, however, rejected their efforts. Later, we see how God begins the process of restoring sacred space.

The ancients believed that certain locations had sacred status, serving as portals through which the gods could travel.

Regarding the confusion of languages, we find in Genesis 10:20 that different languages already existed. In Ancient Near Eastern cultures, kings often forced their subjects to speak a common language in an effort to assimilate captives into their culture. This may have been the case here, and while the confusion of languages was initially disruptive, it also served a restorative purpose: it encouraged the multiplication of people and the filling of the earth. At Pentecost, recorded in Acts 2, we see God reverse the effects of Babel by allowing the Holy Spirit to overcome the language barrier.[32]

In verse 6, the Hebrew text provides some interesting insight. It says that when God looked upon the people, He saw

unity. They were united, speaking a single language—they all spoke as one. But what's wrong with their being united? "All for one, one for all" — isn't this the cry from every pulpit in every church across our land? Unity, unity! In fact, there are groups that harass and bully those who don't agree with them.

The problem is that unity, as mankind defines it, is a false doctrine. Here in Babel, the people had a leader, a vision, and a purpose that they believed was good. Since they all agreed, they had unity. However, when we look at the Scriptures, we don't see God unifying in the way humans often think. More often than not, we see God dividing and separating. What did He do during creation? Later, when Israel ended up in Egypt, God separated them from the Egyptians. When we study the laws of Leviticus, we see God continually instructing the people to separate themselves from the unclean and unholy, and to separate pure from impure things—whether food, animals, or behavior.

Unity itself isn't bad, but the key question is: what or who is the unifying agent? Consensus and compromise are man's type of unity. This is the kind of unity we see throughout the world—people holding hands and declaring they are one. But God's type of unity is different. It's unity in Him. It's each individual holding Christ's hand, and like the hub of a wheel, Christ is the point of unity. This kind of unity has nothing to do with consensus, compromise, or majority rule. In the story of the Tower of Babel, God demonstrated once again how He divides and separates what man tries to unify. And the dividing mechanism He used there was language.

At the birth of the Church, however, we see mankind united in God through the unifying power of the Spirit. In effect,

God was reversing what He had divided and separated over 2,000 years earlier.

Whenever the Bible repeats something, it is for emphasis. In Genesis 4, the root word for "wandering" appears three times in the story of Cain, and here, the root word for "scattered" surfaces three times as well. Both "wandering" and "scattered" vividly capture humanity's plight outside the gates of Eden. As St. Augustine wrote in his *Confessions*, "Our heart is restless until it rests in you."[33] This moment in the narrative is pivotal. Remember, what two things were lost in the fall? Relationship and dominion. From this point onward, God begins the process of restoring that relationship.

Michael Morales writes,

> *Genesis 1–11 narrates humanity's ever-deepening alienation from God, described as an eastward progression away from God's Edenic presence. Included within this account of history, separation from God leads to humanity's increasing ignorance of God. The light of the knowledge of God fades into ever-deepening darkness. Rather than being an innocent lack of understanding, such ignorance becomes the heinous perversion of truth. Although the heavens declare the glory of God, humanity, steeped in the futility of its rebellion, suppresses the memory and knowledge of God. Embracing the offspring of its own faulty thinking, humanity grows ever more ignorant of the living God, fashioning and refashioning*

> *Him into their own fallen image, shaped by twisted desires" (See: Romans 1:18–32).*[34]

As we move away from such a dark period, we should find hope in the words of Vaughan Roberts. In *God's Big Picture*, he references Ephesians 1:3–6:

"Blessed be the God and Father of our Lord Jesus Christ, who has blessed us with every spiritual blessing in the heavenly places in Christ, just as He chose us in Him before the foundation of the world, that we would be holy and blameless before Him. In love He predestined us to adoption as sons through Jesus Christ to Himself, according to the kind intention of His will, to the praise of the glory of His grace, which He freely bestowed on us in the Beloved."

Roberts explains, "Ephesians 1 is mind-blowing in its scope. It takes us from eternity to eternity, from the creation of the world to after its end. The apostle Paul gives us an insight into the eternal plan of God. He is certainly not defeated by the fall. Before the disobedience of Adam and Eve, before they or anything else even existed, God already decided on a rescue plan" (emphasis added).[35]

What God would do was not "Plan B." God knew that man would sin, but He still chose to create him. Imagine getting married and deciding to have children, knowing ahead of time that your children wouldn't just rebel against you but would even want to get rid of you. How likely would you still be to want to have them? That's what Adam and Eve did—they chose to live without needing God. Yet, in His grace, God set out to redeem mankind.

CHAPTER SIX
Abraham

When we left the Perished Kingdom, Adam and Eve had been cast out of the Garden of Eden, sin had progressed to Cain murdering his brother Abel, and humanity became increasingly sinful. In an attempt to regain the "sacred space," people sought to manipulate God by constructing a tower for Him to descend. Alongside this tower, they built a temple they considered "sacred space." However, it was not truly sacred because it was not occupied by Yahweh, the God of the Bible. The flood marked the moment when God disrupted this disordered state and began humanity's journey back toward sacred space.

In Genesis 1-11, the focus is on humanity: the beginning of human history and the root of the problem. In Genesis 11:29, we are introduced to Abram and his wife, Sarai. The story immediately begins on a somber note: verse 30 states, "Sarai was barren." This detail is significant because it contrasts with the blessing given to Adam, which was associated with fertility. Sarai's infertility highlights the brokenness of humanity. In Genesis 12-50, the narrative shifts to focus on Abraham (Abram) and his descendants. This section marks the beginning of Hebrew history and demonstrates that the purpose of Abraham's lineage is to benefit the entire world.[1] This is also the beginning of the solution to the problem introduced in earlier chapters.

Who is Abram? His story begins in a rather unexpected place: the city of Ur of the Chaldees. Archaeological discoveries have identified Ur as a city that was likely henotheistic. To clarify, polytheism involves the worship of many gods, monotheism involves the worship of only one God, and henotheism involves the worship of one primary god while acknowledging the existence of others. In Ur, people worshipped the moon god but believed in the existence of other deities. If you lived there, it is highly probable you would have been a moon worshipper.

In this cultural context, gods were believed to control every aspect of life. Whether events were good or bad, the gods were seen as the cause. Life revolved around keeping these deities happy. People often had personal gods, minor deities known as patron gods, who were believed to offer individual guidance or protection.

When Abram encountered Yahweh, it may have seemed to others that Abram had simply acquired a new god. It is possible that Abram initially regarded Yahweh as his personal god while still recognizing the existence of other gods. Alternatively, Abram may have come to realize that the gods worshipped by the people of Ur were not real. This encounter with Yahweh marked a pivotal moment, setting Abram apart and beginning the story of a relationship with the one true God, Yahweh.

God's Call and Covenant

Why does God call Abram? He is in the line of the blessing. The genealogies of Adam, Seth, and Noah bring us to Abram. The word "blessing" occurs five times in three verses, contrasting the five curses mentioned in Genesis 3:11-40.[2] God tells him, *"Go forth from your country, and from your relatives, and from your father's house."* He is being told to leave everything familiar to him. He is also leaving his old deities, who are tied to his city or family. In doing so, Abram breaks all religious ties and begins to see Yahweh as his personal God. Later, Yahweh will become more than a personal god; He will be known as the God of Abraham, Isaac, and Jacob.

What stands out about Abram is his entrepreneurial spirit. What does it take to be an entrepreneur? There is a risk, cost, determination, perseverance through difficulties, criticism from others, great reward when successful, and admiration from others. If Abram had told people what he was doing and why, one could have imagined the criticism he would face. He likely knew very little about the world beyond the lush Mesopotamian valley where he had lived his entire life.

Significantly, Yahweh spoke to Abram. The gods of Ur never spoke to him. Yahweh also promised to fulfill Abram's deepest desires: family, land, and fame. While the builders of Babel sought to make a name for themselves, God promised to make Abram's name great and to build him into a nation that would bless the entire world.[3] Leon Kass, a Jewish scholar, notes that Yahweh's promises directly address Abram's deepest longings—prosperity, family, and legacy.[4]

It is crucial to understand that Abram is blessed not for his own sake but to be a blessing to all nations. At this stage, Yahweh only asks Abram to go. There are no other immediate demands. Similarly, God calls us to take a step of faith and obedience when we accept Him as our Savior.

At this point, Abram is childless, rootless, homeless, and probably godless. He is destined to become a wanderer.

In Genesis 12:1-7, God establishes a grant covenant with Abram. To fully grasp its significance, we must first understand the concept of a covenant. The Hebrew word for covenant is *berit*, which refers to a solemn, binding arrangement between two parties, entailing various responsibilities, benefits, and penalties.[5] Sandra Richter, in her book *Epic of Eden*, categorizes covenants into individual, tribal, or national levels. For instance, Abraham makes an individual covenant with his servant in Genesis 24, Isaac makes a tribal covenant with Abimelech in Genesis 26, and Joshua makes a national covenant with the Gibeonites in Joshua 9-10.[6]

Richter further explains that covenants often involved the concept of "fictive kinship," where a non-relative was legally bound to care for another as if they were family.[7] By claiming someone biologically unrelated as kin, one establishes a binding relationship of privilege and responsibility.[8]

The covenant God makes with Abram in Genesis 12 is known as a grant covenant. This type of covenant differs from the treaty-style covenant ratified in Genesis 15. As John Walton explains:

> *While the "treaty" constitutes an obligation of the vassal to his master, the suzerain, the "grant"*

> *constitutes an obligation of the master to his servant. In the "grant," the curse is directed toward those who violate the servant's rights, whereas in the treaty, the curse is directed toward the vassal who violates the master's rights. In other words, the "grant" primarily protects the servant's rights, while the treaty protects the master's. Moreover, the grant is a reward for loyalty already demonstrated, whereas the treaty is an inducement for future loyalty.*[9]

Evidence of grant covenants in the Ancient Near East can be found on kudurru stones, which served as boundary markers. These markers were used when governments lacked sufficient authority to guarantee private property rights.[10] Divine curses and the witness of the gods were invoked to protect these grants, especially in hostile territories.[11] Royal seals authenticated the grants, and kings pledged their power to uphold them.[12] Dynastic succession was tied to land ownership, as the granted land became the property of the recipient's family.[13]

In Genesis 12, Yahweh makes a grant covenant with Abram, establishing a relationship between a king (Yahweh) and a loyal subject (Abram) sent to settle in a hostile land (Canaan). Yahweh promises to curse those who curse Abram and to give him land for himself and his descendants. However, there is an apparent problem with this promise: Abram and Sarai are childless, and Sarai is barren. Since being blessed involves fertility, this creates tension in the narrative. We might think of this grant covenant as an engagement before marriage—a reward for Abram's faithfulness and a prelude to the fuller covenant to come.

Trials and Divine Encounters

Abram's journey will be shaped by eleven tests or trials, ten divine encounters, and four divine actions he knows nothing about.[14] The first test and divine encounter occur when Yahweh tells Abram to "go." All of Abram's trials involve faith and obedience.

In Genesis 12:12, Abram is referred to as a sojourner. A sojourner, or alien, is someone living in a land without civil rights.[15] Why does Lot go with Abram? One reason is that Lot's father has died, and Abram assumes responsibility for protecting Lot's civil rights. This dynamic mirrors Israel's exodus from Egypt, where others joined them. Similarly, those who are not part of the blessing sometimes benefit by associating with those who are. Outsiders can become insiders, and insiders can become outsiders depending on their actions.

Second Divine Encounter and Test

Abram's second encounter with God occurs in Genesis 12:7, where Yahweh promises to give Abram's descendants the land of Canaan. His second test comes in Genesis 12:11-16 when he travels to Egypt. Here, Abram learns what it means to be treated unjustly as a stranger.[16] Abram, fearing for his life because of Sarai's beauty, tells her in verse 11 to lie and claim she is his sister:

"See now, I know that you are a beautiful woman, and when the Egyptians see you, they will say, 'This is his wife'; and they will kill me, but they will let you live. Please say that you are my sister so that it may go well with me because of you and that I may live on account of you."

Abram's actions may shock us, but cultural factors shed light on his reasoning. First, even though Abram feared God, he did not rely on his own merit. He believed that through Sarai's merit, he would be protected and prosper. Second, genealogical records show that Sarai was Abram's niece, and nieces and nephews were often considered "siblings" in Ancient Near Eastern cultures. By presenting Sarai as his sister, Abram hoped to avoid death and force Pharaoh to negotiate with him. Third, as a sojourner without civil rights, Abram acted out of self-preservation, possibly doubting Yahweh's power in a foreign land.[17]

Third Test and Divine Encounter

The third test occurs in Genesis 13 when disputes arise between Abram's and Lot's herdsmen. Abram gives Lot the choice of land, and Lot selects the fertile plains of Sodom and Gomorrah, seeking paradise in exile.[18] Abram's test is to trust Yahweh to provide the land He promised. After Lot departs, God reiterates His promise to Abram, marking the third divine encounter.

Fourth Test and Divine Encounter

In Genesis 14, Lot and his family are captured during a conflict, and Abram must decide whether to fulfill his familial obligation to rescue them. This test highlights Abram's loyalty and courage. After defeating the captors, Abram meets Melchizedek, the "king of Salem" and "priest of God Most High," who blesses Abram. Abram gives him a tithe, recognizing his spiritual authority. Hebrews 7:1-3 later describes Melchizedek as a figure resembling the Son of God, sparking debates about his identity. This encounter is widely regarded as Abram's fourth divine encounter.

Chapter 15 shows a significant development of the relationship between Yahweh and mankind. Yahweh has promised Abram children, and he wants God to fulfill that promise. He asks Yahweh if Eliezer of Damascus, his faithful steward, will end up with everything. In verse four, Yahweh begins to respond. Yahweh promises Abram descendants.

> *The literal word used here is "seed." Unfortunately, the word is often rendered "descendants" or "offspring." This word occurs fifty-nine times in Genesis, compared to one hundred and seventy times in the rest of the Old Testament. Several factors are worth noting briefly about the use of the term "seed" in Genesis. First, the Hebrew word* zera*ʿ can be either singular or plural, like the English word "sheep"; it may denote a single seed or many seeds. Second, "seed" normally denotes an individual's natural child or children. Third, the Hebrew word* zera*ʿ conveys the idea that there is a close resemblance between the seed and that which has produced it. We see this un-*

> *derlying the comment that plants and trees are to produce seeds "according to their various kinds" (1: 11–12).*[19]

This is the fourth divine encounter, and Yahweh ratifies His covenant with Abram. There is a marked change in the covenant. As I said earlier, the grant covenant was like an engagement–this is more like a marriage. This is what was known as a suzerain and vassal covenant. This type of covenant was used between nations. The more powerful nation would be the suzerain, and the weaker nation would be the vassal. The suzerain could demand the submission of the vassal. They often referred to each other as either "father and son" or "lord and servant."[20] There were requirements in this covenant, and a suzerain may have several vassal nations that were subject to it, but a vassal could not have more than one suzerain because loyalty was considered to be most important. The term in the Bible that best describes this sort of loyalty is *hesed*, which is "covenant faithfulness."[21] We have seen the grant covenant, which was a reward for faithfulness. Now, we are witnessing a suzerain and vassal covenant, which is like a treaty and is more concerned with the vassal's obligations toward the suzerain. The book of Deuteronomy and the New Testament tell us to love the LORD with all our hearts. Ashurbanipal, a 7th century B.C. Assyrian king wrote to one of his vassals, "You shall love Ashurbanipal, king of Assyria, your lord, as yourself. You shall hearken to whatever he says and do whatever he commands, and you shall not seek any other king or lord against him."[22]

We will see that every suzerain-vassal covenant had three elements. Verses 5 and 7 are the first element of the covenant—

a promise. He promises descendants and land. A second element in the suzerain-vassal covenant is the requirements. We see the requirements in verse 6. *"Then he believed in the LORD, and He reckoned it to him as righteousness."* Yahweh will add to this later. In verse 8, Abram wants some assurance of what Yahweh has promised. He is told to get some animals, split them in half, and arrange them opposite each other. He is not told to do that with the animals, but he knows what to do. This was a common covenant practice. In verse 11, Abram chases the birds away. To a person ANE, there was nothing worse than to be killed and your body left exposed for the birds to devour. Marty Solomon of Campus Ministries says,

> *[He is]setting up what is called a blood path covenant. This is a covenant sign that is often used in Abram's day to signify a betrothal (engagement) covenant. Those animals are used, cut in half, and arranged opposite one another on opposing slopes. The arranged halves create a path of blood between the animals. I will use the example of a betrothal to explain the ceremony. As the two parties agree to the marriage, the lesser party (in the example, this would be the future groom; he is asking the father of the future bride to marry his daughter) dons a white robe and then passes through the path of blood. As the blood splashes up on his white robe, the symbolic statement is, "If I mistreat or abuse your daughter, you may do this in my blood." After this, the father dons*

> *a white robe and passes through the blood path, saying, "If I do not supply you with a virgin for a daughter, you may do this in my blood.*[23]

God puts Abram in a deep sleep (the same sleep He put Adam in, by the way), and while Abram is greatly distressed and troubled, Abram sees a flaming torch and smoking pot pass between the halves. Fire and smoke always symbolize the presence of God (think the pillar of fire/smoke). So what does Abram see? God is passing through the covenant halves—twice. God passes through the halves on behalf of Abram. Jeremiah 34:18-20 refers to this same practice of a covenant made by cutting animals and repeating the oath of the covenant as one walks through the animal parts. John Stott said, "It may truly be said without exaggeration that not only the rest of the Old Testament but the whole of the New Testament are an outworking of these promises of God."[24]

Fifth Test

In Genesis 16, we encounter Abraham's fifth test. Sarai, desperate for children, speaks for the first time in this chapter. Abram, acting on her suggestion, takes matters into his own hands and fathers a child with Sarai's maidservant, Hagar. Hagar gives birth to Ishmael. This decision will have long-lasting negative consequences, as Ishmael's descendants became known as the Arabs—people with whom Israel continues to have conflicts today. There is an interesting parallel between this incident and an earlier one in Egypt, when Abram allowed

Pharaoh to take Sarai as his wife. Now, Sarai urges Abram to take the Egyptian bondwoman, Hagar.[25]

Fifth Divine Encounter and Sixth Test

In Chapter 17, Abram experiences his fifth divine encounter. God changes his name to Abraham, meaning "father of many" or "father of a multitude." Sarai's name is also changed to Sarah, meaning "princess." The significance of names in the Bible is rooted in the creation story, where naming something signified authority over it. It also conveyed a person's identity, as seen later with Jacob, whose name changes reflect his life's trajectory. Abraham's new name reflects his future role as the father not only of Israel but also of Christianity.

There is another layer to the change of names. In biblical times, when a woman married, she typically adopted her husband's name. Likewise, God's renaming of Abram and Sarai signifies a deeper bond. In verse 1, God reveals a new name for Himself—El Shaddai, meaning "God Almighty." This marks a moment of mutual identity between God and Abraham. The addition of the Hebrew letter "heh" (Y-H-W-H) to Abram's name signifies that he will be "the father of a multitude of nations."[26]

It is also in this encounter that Yahweh commands Abraham to follow Him wholeheartedly, meaning to align his ways with God's.[27] Abraham responds in complete surrender by falling on his face in submission.

The divine encounter is followed by the sixth test, circumcision, introduced in verse 23. The sign of the covenant, circumcision, signifies, "If I fail to keep the covenant, I will be cut off from the community." This implies being excluded from the covenant promises. Humanity can only live as God intended when the flesh is put to death. Since the fall, mankind has acted based on its own understanding of good and evil rather than God's will. In opposing the flesh, Yahweh is not rejecting humanity but working to deliver it from everything that makes people act in a more animalistic way. In His struggle against the flesh, Yahweh is also confronting pride.

The covenant of circumcision is given in the context of God's promise of an abundant seed (Gen. 17:16) that will inherit and inhabit the land He promises. Circumcision signifies that Abraham's descendants will not inherit the land by human strength, military might, or heroism. While God promises fertility, He also shows that Abraham will father the promised seed only when he surrenders his hope in the flesh.

It is significant that Abram could father the promised child, Isaac, only after undergoing circumcision. Sarah's pregnancy with Isaac occurs only after Abraham has undergone the procedure. Circumcision plays a pivotal role in redirecting human history, just as the original call for Abraham to leave his homeland did. Sarah, at the age of 90, conceives as part of Abraham's entry into the sacred covenant. Additionally, Sarah's name is changed from "Sarai" to "Sarah" with the addition of the letter "heh," symbolizing that Isaac is not a product of human effort but a miraculous act of Yahweh.[28]

Sixth Divine Encounter and Seventh Test

Genesis 18 describes Abraham's sixth divine encounter and his seventh test, which involves the visit of three angels. This encounter focuses on the theme of hospitality. How will Abraham treat strangers? How will he respond to those who are different from himself? In the desert, hospitality is not only a necessity but also highly esteemed. It is considered sacred. A guest could rely on this hospitality for up to three days, and even after departing, they were entitled to protection for a certain period, which varied between tribes.[29] One tribe, for example, stated that the protection lasted "until the salt he has eaten has left his stomach." This practice is significant, and we will see its importance shortly.

Abraham demonstrates hospitality by treating strangers with great respect, preparing a meal for them, and showing kindness to those who are unfamiliar to him.

Eighth Test and Seventh Divine Encounter

In the seventh divine encounter, God tells Abraham that he will have a son by this time next year. Sarah overhears this and laughs, so the child is to be named Isaac, which means "laughter." The three angels then inform Abraham that God will destroy Sodom and Gomorrah. In response, Abraham attempts to negotiate with God, reducing the number of righteous people needed to spare the cities, starting with 50, then 45, 40, 30, 20, and finally 10. He likely stops there, having pushed the negotiation as far as he feels he can.

Verse 22 is noteworthy because two of the angels proceed to Sodom while the Lord remains with Abraham, suggesting that the third angel might be the Lord Himself. This marks the eighth test for Abraham as he pleads for the fate of a wicked city. Abraham questions whether God will destroy the righteous along with the wicked. Through this encounter, Abraham demonstrates his morality and compassion while also gaining a deeper understanding of divine justice.

In Genesis 19, the men of Sodom attempt to assault the angels sent by God, and Lot tries to prevent this act. The angels strike the men with blindness. This episode highlights the significance of Abraham's passing the test of hospitality. The actions of the men of Sodom represent a profound indignity—they attempt to dominate and humiliate their guests. In the ancient world, offering hospitality was a sacred duty, and it was the host's responsibility to ensure the safety of their guests. Lot makes the ultimate sacrifice by offering his daughters to the mob in order to protect his guests, demonstrating the immense value of hospitality.

A lack of hospitality reflects a disdain for those who are different. In contrast, sodomy is rooted in a desire for the familiar and an aversion to the unfamiliar. It is an expression of selfishness and a rejection of procreation, directly opposing God's command to Adam and Noah to *"be fruitful and multiply."* It shifts the focus from fulfilling the divine mandate to indulging in selfish pleasures. Remember, God created sexuality to be complementary.[30]

In Israel, homosexuality was considered a capital offense. When the Israelites leave Egypt, they are instructed in Exodus 23:9, "You must not oppress foreigners. You know what it's like to be a foreigner, for you yourselves were once foreigners in the land of Egypt." The promise made to Abraham was to bless all nations, and as mentioned earlier, outsiders will become insiders. Now, let's return to the story.

The angels forcefully remove Lot, his wife, and daughters from the city before God destroys Sodom and Gomorrah. As they flee, Lot's wife looks back and turns into a pillar of salt. Why did God do this? Because she disobeyed the divine command not to look back. When we look back at our past, it signifies that we have not fully left it behind emotionally.

Lot's daughters, fearing they would remain without husbands, made their father drunk in order to have children by him. The availability of husbands was limited, and this act resulted in the genealogy of the Moabites and Ammonites. These two groups will become significant in the history of Canaan and cause trouble for the Hebrews. However, one Moabite will later play a pivotal role in Israel and Christianity: Ruth, who will be included in the genealogies of David and Jesus.

We might wonder why God didn't punish the daughters. It's important to remember that this was an ancient culture where certain actions were more accepted. Moreover, this occurred long before the formal establishment of the Mosaic law.

In Genesis 20, we encounter the ninth test, where Abraham again lies about Sarah being his sister. It's remarkable—Sarah is 99 years old, yet Abimelech desires her. She must have been extraordinarily beautiful if she remained attractive at that age. Some believe that Abimelech might have wanted Sarah for political and economic alliances with Abraham.

Interestingly, in verse 9, God speaks to Abimelech, revealing that what Abraham did was sinful. Abimelech calls Abraham a "prophet," meaning he is seen as someone who speaks on behalf of God, implying that Abraham has a significant connection to God. Notice that the Bible doesn't shy away from showing the flaws of God's people.

The consequences of Abimelech taking Sarah were severe: all the women in his household became barren. In the ancient world, fertility was considered a sign of divine blessing, while infertility was a curse. Ultimately, Abraham prays for Abimelech, and God restores the women's fertility.

Finally, in Genesis 21, the promised son, Isaac, is born. Abraham is 100, and Sarah is 99. This shows us that God does things completely beyond our capabilities. Ishmael was what Abraham and Hagar could do; Isaac was not. Why does God insist on the promise coming through Isaac? In Galatians 4:21-28 the apostle Paul explains:

> *Tell me, you who want to be under law, do you not listen to the law?*
>
> *22 For it is written that Abraham had two sons, one by the bondwoman and one by the free woman.*
>
> *23 But the son by the bondwoman was born according to the flesh, and the son by the free woman through the promise.*

24 *This is allegorically speaking, for these women are two covenants: one proceeding from Mount Sinai bearing children who are to be slaves; she is Hagar.*

25 *Now this Hagar is Mount Sinai in Arabia and corresponds to the present Jerusalem, for she is in slavery with her children.*

26 *But the Jerusalem above is free; she is our mother.*

27 *For it is written,*

"REJOICE, BARREN WOMAN WHO DOES NOT BEAR;

BREAK FORTH AND SHOUT, YOU WHO ARE NOT IN LABOR;

FOR MORE NUMEROUS ARE THE CHILDREN OF THE DESOLATE

THAN OF THE ONE WHO HAS A HUSBAND."

28 *And you, brethren, like Isaac, are children of promise.*

Eighth Divine Encounter and Tenth Test

In Genesis 21, Sarah insists that Hagar and Ishmael be sent away, which deeply upsets Abraham. Perhaps he views Ishmael as his firstborn and is reluctant to part with him. However,

God speaks to Abraham and tells him to follow Sarah's request, emphasizing that there should be no contest for the blessing. It's striking that, despite forcing Hagar and Ishmael to leave, God still shows great care for this Egyptian bondwoman.

In verses 15–18, we read how Hagar and Ishmael find themselves in the wilderness, running out of water—an absolutely desperate situation. In her despair, Hagar leaves Ishmael under a bush to die. But God takes notice of them, provides water, and promises that Ishmael will become a great nation. While this may seem like an isolated incident, it offers a profound lesson. If God shows such mercy to Hagar, will He not also care for Israel when they are in the desert? As someone once said, "What God has done in the past is a model and a promise of what He will do in the future, but He is too creative to do it the same way."

Ninth and Tenth Divine Encounters and Eleventh Test

In Genesis 22, we reach the final two divine encounters and the supreme test. God commands Abraham to sacrifice Isaac. This is the ultimate test of Abraham's faith—whether he values God's gifts more than he values God Himself. In Chapter 12, God asked Abraham to leave behind his past; here, He asks Abraham to relinquish his future.

Interestingly, in the Ancient Near East (ANE), the god El was associated with fertility and had the right to demand a portion of that fertility as a sacrifice. Abraham would have been familiar with child sacrifice, so this command was not entirely foreign to him. However, the key point here is how Abraham responds to God's command—he does so without hesitation.

It is significant that Abraham must travel for three days, all the while contemplating the act of sacrificing his promised son. Jesus, too, was dead for three days. Abraham journeys to Mount Moriah, the future site of Solomon's Temple. He is instructed not only to sacrifice Isaac but to offer him as a burnt offering. The burnt offering, also called an "ascension offering," involved the smoke of the offering rising to God. This act was not merely symbolic; the offering was actually transformed from something solid into smoke, ascending to God.

As they climb the mountain, Abraham makes a remarkable statement in verse 5: "We will worship and return." Isaac, approximately 17 years old and strong enough to resist his father, carries the wood for the altar. He expresses concern, noticing that they have everything for the sacrifice except the animal. Abraham reassures him in verse 8, saying, *"God will provide."* When they reach the summit, Abraham arranges the wood on the altar, binds Isaac, and raises the knife to sacrifice him. At the last moment, in verse 11, God calls, *"Abraham, Abraham."* It is here that Abraham's love for God is proven to surpass his love for God's gifts.

This is the first instance in Scripture where a substitutionary sacrifice is made—the ram dies in Isaac's place. God also reveals His name as Jehovah-Jireh, meaning "The LORD Provides." Abraham, who once saw God as his patron, now learns that God is the provider. As God continues to reveal Himself to the Hebrew people, He will be known by many other names.

As mentioned earlier concerning the idea of "seed" being plural and singular, we note in verse 18 that the word refers

specifically to Isaac. "Genesis anticipates that a royal descendant from Abraham will play an important role in bringing divine blessing to all the nations of earth."[31]

What does Abraham's life teach us about the relationship between faith and works? God makes the promise, but Abraham's obedience is required for him to receive it.

Interestingly, while the text notes that Abraham returns, Isaac is not mentioned. One Jewish writer suggests that Isaac's relationship with his father was strained because of the traumatic experience. In fact, Abraham and Isaac will not appear together again until Chapter 25:9, when they bury Abraham. In 24:67, Isaac grieves the loss of his mother, but there is no mention of him grieving the death of his father. Isaac may have believed that his father's actions were wrong, leading to a rupture in their relationship.[32]

Sarah's Death

In Genesis 23, we learn of Sarah's death, and Abraham purchases land to bury her. This scene is portrayed as a legal transaction, taking place at the city gate with witnesses present. Typically, the sale of land was restricted within the family, as land represented the ability to provide for one's group through crops. Daniel Snell argues that "fields could be sold only to relatives closely related through males."[33]

The elders of the area vouch for Abraham, calling him a "prince," which indicates his status as a desirable neighbor. Abraham asks the "sons of Heth" to sell him a burial site. They offer the land as a gift, but he refuses, knowing that accepting it as a gift would allow the owner's heirs to reclaim it later. The haggling over the price shows that the seller sees Abraham as someone in need and seeks to take advantage of the situation. Abraham ends up paying a high price for the land.

While this may seem like a minor detail, it marks an important shift: Abraham now owns property in the land, signaling that he is no longer an outsider but a citizen of the land that will one day be known as Israel.

A Wife for Isaac

In Genesis 24, Abraham sends his trusted servant, Eliezer, back to Mesopotamia to find a wife for Isaac. Recall that earlier, Abraham had wondered if Eliezer would inherit everything upon his death. Now, Abraham is fulfilling his patriarchal duty: Isaac must not marry a Canaanite woman. Abraham makes Eliezer swear an oath, and to seal it, he has Eliezer place his hand under Abraham's thigh. This action, though unusual, symbolizes the seriousness of the oath. The thigh is near the reproductive organs, so the gesture corresponds to the covenant of future generations, ensuring that Abraham's descendants will fulfill the promise.

Eliezer travels back to the land of Abraham's ancestors, heading west—always a direction associated with returning to sacred space, as opposed to the east, which symbolizes departure from it.

At a well, Eliezer meets Rebekah, the granddaughter of Abraham's brother, which is significant both for the family connection and because wells were social gathering places. As we'll see in later stories, Jacob meets his wife at a well, Moses meets his wife at a well, and Jesus encounters the woman at the well. Wells served as places where people, particularly women, found husbands, much like social hubs today.

Eliezer employs a common practice in the Ancient Near East known as a "mechanistic oracle," where someone asks a deity a yes-no question to reveal God's will. Eliezer's question concerns finding the right wife for Isaac. His specific test involves asking a woman for a drink of water. Offering a drink was customary, but Eliezer asks for something beyond the norm—he requests that the woman not only give him water but also provide water for all ten of his camels. This would be an extraordinary task, as each camel can drink up to 25 gallons of water, and the typical water jug at the time held 3 gallons.[34] Rebekah's willingness to take on this enormous task is a sign of divine providence.

Rebekah's family recognizes that this encounter is orchestrated by God. In verse 22, when Eliezer places bracelets on Rebekah's arms, it symbolizes a marriage contract. The bracelets weigh ten shekels, equivalent to a year's wage for a worker. Eliezer recounts how Abraham instructed him to find a wife for Isaac and how Rebekah fulfilled the test.

Interestingly, Rebekah has no direct say in the decision to go with Eliezer to marry Isaac. This decision rests with her father, who will ultimately determine her fate.

Isaac and Rebekah's Marriage

In Genesis 24:53, Eliezer gives the family lavish gifts, showcasing Abraham's great wealth. These gifts serve as a reward for accepting the marriage proposal. Once the marriage agreement is made, Eliezer presents jewels and fine clothing for Rebekah, along with valuable gifts for her father and mother. This practice is reminiscent of the mohar, a bridal payment mentioned in Genesis 34:12 (which we will explore in another chapter). The mohar was paid by the fiancé to the bride's father, and the amount varied depending on the father's status and the family's social standing.[35]

In verse 55, Rebekah's family requests that Eliezer wait for ten days. This delay likely serves to ensure that everything is as it appears and that no hasty decisions are made. Rebekah, trusting her family's protection, agrees to leave.[36] When they ask Rebekah if she will go with Eliezer, she responds affirmatively: "Yes, I will go." Typically, a girl wasn't asked for her consent in such matters. The reason Rebekah is asked may be because her father has passed, and her brother is now acting in the role of authority.[37]

Interestingly, Rebekah leaves her home and kin to journey to a land much like Abraham's own. In verse 60, her family blesses her, wishing her to "become the mother of millions," echoing the promise God made to Abraham. Although the Bible doesn't describe the marriage ceremony in detail, verse 65 gives us a glimpse of the customs.

> *The chief ceremony was the bride's entry into the bridegroom's house. The bridegroom, wearing a diadem and accompanied by friends with tambourines and a band, proceeded to the bride's house. She was richly dressed and adorned with*

> *jewels, but she wore a veil, which she took off only in the bridal chamber. This explains why Rebekah veiled herself upon seeing Issac.*[38]

Isaac marries Rebekah, and it becomes clear that Rebekah, rather than Isaac, plays a pivotal role in protecting the promise. Abraham has shown throughout his life that he always obeys God's commands, and now Rebekah, too, shows faithfulness in following the divine plan.

In Genesis 25, Abraham dies at 175.

We can learn three things about faith from Abraham. First, walking with God isn't always comfortable. Secondly, you cannot discover new oceans unless you have the courage to lose sight of the shore. Finally, moving forward with God sometimes requires leaving something behind.

How will Issac respond to his patriarchal responsibilities, and how will he demonstrate his faithfulness to Yahweh? That is what we will see next.

CHAPTER SEVEN
Isaac

As we transition from the narratives of Abraham and Isaac, the formation of the Hebrew people and the nation of Israel remains on the horizon. While Isaac's life may seem relatively uneventful compared to his father's, it is pivotal in advancing the fulfillment of Abraham's blessing. Kass observes:

> *Abraham, in fact, had a rather distinguished career in international relations. He escaped the danger in Egypt, won a military victory against invading Babylonian kings, participated in God's judgment against Sodom and Gomorrah, established a pact of friendship with Abimelech and the Philistines, and purchased burial land from the Hittites...Isaac [is] much more limited in scope than his father.*[1]

In Genesis 25, Abraham dies at the age of 175, and the focus shifts to Isaac's family. His wife, Rebekah, initially struggles with barrenness—a recurring theme in the patriarchal narratives that underscores God's intervention in fulfilling His promises. After fervent prayer, Rebekah becomes pregnant, and verses 21-26 recount the birth of their twin sons, Jacob and Esau. This marks a critical juncture in the story as the narrative begins to explore their differences and their roles in the unfolding of God's plan.

God's Choice

Just as God would not allow the blessing to be given to Ishmael, the younger is to inherit the blessing, as God instructs Rebekah in what is known as an oracle in verse 23: An oracle is:

> *Communications from God. The term refers both to divine responses to a question asked of God and to pronouncements made by God without His being asked. In one sense, oracles were prophecies since they often referred to the future; but oracles sometimes dealt with decisions to be made in the present. Usually, in the Bible, the communication was from Yahweh, the God of Israel. In times of idol worship, however, Israelites did seek a word or pronouncement from false gods. (Hosea 4:12)*[2]

Yahweh says, *"The older shall serve the younger."* Although Jacob and Esau are twins, they look nothing alike. Interestingly, in the culture of the Ancient Near East (ANE), the oldest son would traditionally inherit the major portion of his father's estate and assume the family's leadership responsibilities. However, God declares that this will not happen in this case, breaking the expected cultural norms. This pattern of God's favor bypassing the eldest recurs throughout the Old Testament.

Paul reflects on this divine choice in Romans 9:10-12: *"And not only this, but there was Rebekah also, when she had conceived twins by one man, our father Isaac; for though the twins were not yet born and had not done anything good or bad, so that God's purpose according to His choice would stand, not because of works but because of Him who calls."* Iain Duguid emphasizes the significance of God's choice: "God wants to make it clear from the start that there is no favoritism with Him. There are no privileged positions in God's family. Being born of Abraham is not enough; being born of Isaac and Rebekah is not enough; being the oldest child is not enough.... He chooses the unfavored younger sons who have neither status nor strength to show that all is of grace from start to finish."[3]

Esau, whose name means "hairy," is a hunter, and Jacob is a homebody. Esau is later called Edom, which means "red," and points to his abundant body hair and red complexion.[4] He will be the father of the Amalekites, who attack Israel as they come out of Egypt later. When they are born, Jacob holds Esau's ankle as though trying to keep Esau from being born first so he could claim the birthright. Jacob's name means "He grasps the heel," "trickster," or "supplanter."[5]

As the story unfolds, one day Esau returns from hunting, hungry and exhausted, to find Jacob cooking stew. In verse 30, Esau demands some of what Jacob has prepared. The verb phrase "let me have" can be translated as "let me gulp down" and is typically used for feeding animals, suggesting a crude, almost desperate demeanor. Notably, the Hebrew Bible often portrays its characters speaking eloquently, making Esau's blunt request stand out—almost as if a Shakespearean character suddenly spoke like a New York taxi driver. This moment foreshadows Esau's impulsive nature and lack of foresight.[6]

Esau's impulsive decision to sell his birthright reveals deeper character flaws. The birthright, as the firstborn, would have entitled him to a double portion of Isaac's inheritance and the authority to lead the family after Isaac's death. Yet, driven by immediate gratification, Esau dismisses its significance. His actions parallel humanity's tendency to prioritize temporary desires over lasting blessings, a theme first seen in the Garden of Eden with Eve's choice to follow her appetites. Jacob does not deceive Esau in this transaction; rather, Esau's disregard for his birthright demonstrates his own lack of reverence for the blessing. Witnessed by other shepherds, the transaction is legally binding, underscoring the weight of Esau's decision.

Jacob is described as "peaceful," but the term is somewhat ambiguous and often translated as "quiet." More precisely, it conveys the idea of being "single-minded" or "single-hearted," carrying connotations of a person with high moral character. It describes someone whose desires and actions are fully aligned, much like the root of the English word *integrity* suggests.[7] Ironically, Jacob will soon demonstrate behavior that is far from this ideal.

In Genesis 26, the narrative shifts back to Isaac. In verses 3–5, God blesses Jacob in a manner reminiscent of Abraham's blessing. Like Abraham, Isaac faces a dilemma with a Gerarite concerning his wife. Following his father's example, Isaac lies about Rebekah, claiming she is his sister. As the saying goes, "The fruit doesn't fall far from the tree." However, Abimelech observes Isaac being affectionate with Rebekah and confronts him. Thanks to Abimelech's integrity, Isaac and Rebekah's marriage remains protected.

Some scholars suggest that this episode may have occurred before the birth of Jacob and Esau, as having children would have made Isaac's claim about Rebekah more difficult to believe. Alternatively, it could have taken place after the boys had grown and Isaac relocated to Gerar.[8]

In Gerar, Isaac stands out as the first and only successful farmer mentioned in Genesis. His prosperity grows so significantly that the Philistines become envious and fearful of his power. To distance themselves from him, they sabotage his success by stopping up all his wells. When Isaac digs new wells, the locals claim ownership, leading to further disputes. As a result, Isaac continually moves away.

Why doesn't Isaac fight for the wells? The answer lies in verse 3: he is a sojourner and holds no civil rights in Gerar. In the absence of precise laws, disputes over wells or cisterns were common. It was generally understood which watering places belonged to which group, but this informal system left Isaac vulnerable. Consequently, he is driven out repeatedly.[9]

Finally, in verse 22, Isaac digs a well without opposition. He names the place Rehoboth, meaning "open spaces," signifying relief and the hope of flourishing without conflict.

In verses 23–25, God reaffirms the covenant He made with Abraham. Isaac responds by performing three significant acts:

1. He builds an altar and calls on the name of the LORD, signifying the holiness of the place.
2. He pitches a tent, an act symbolizing his claim on the land.
3. He digs a well, further solidifying his presence and taking possession of the land.

These last two actions are especially noteworthy because they mark a shift in Isaac's status—he is no longer merely a sojourner.

Later, in verses 28–29, Abimelech approaches Isaac to establish a covenant. This covenant reflects a relationship of equality, rather than a suzerain-vassal dynamic. Abimelech and his people acknowledge Isaac as *"blessed of the LORD,"* recognizing him not just as an individual but as a national entity.

The Patriarchal Blessing

In Genesis 27, the narrative shifts back to Jacob and Esau. Isaac, now old and nearly blind, seeks to put his house in order. Interestingly, Esau is Isaac's favorite, seemingly because they share similar traits. Like Esau, Isaac is a man influenced by his appetites. Esau sold his birthright for a bowl of stew, and Isaac requested food before bestowing the blessing. This pattern underscores Isaac's preoccupation with physical desires.[10] In contrast, when Abraham was old, he prioritized securing a proper wife for Isaac, but Isaac had neglected to ensure the same for his sons. His focus is on eating, even as he prepares to pronounce the blessing—a ritual often accompanied by a celebratory meal.[11]

Rebekah, however, has received an oracle from the LORD and knows which son is meant to inherit the blessing. Determined to align events with God's intention, she intervenes to ensure Jacob receives it.[12] Allowing Esau to be blessed would contradict God's plan. It's worth noting that Rebekah is Laban's sister, a relationship that foreshadows her cunning actions. Following her instructions, Jacob deceives his father. Dressed in Esau's clothes to mimic his brother's smell and feel, Jacob capitalizes on Isaac's failing senses. Isaac cannot discern between Esau's wild game and Rebekah's cooking, and he unknowingly bestows the blessing on Jacob.

The story emphasizes the significance of the blessing through repetition: the word *blessing* appears seven times, and its verbal form occurs twenty-one times—three times seven.[13] This covenantal blessing includes fertile land, dominion over nations (including siblings), and a reciprocal effect for curses and blessings. However, it resembles the blessings of a *grant covenant* rather than a covenant with Yahweh; there is no mention of land, descendants, or a direct relationship with God.[14] This distinction highlights Isaac's character: while Abraham obeyed God without question, Isaac appears willing to act pragmatically to achieve his desires.

When Isaac realizes he has blessed Jacob instead of Esau, verse 33 describes him trembling—a moment of profound realization. For the first time since Abraham nearly sacrificed him on Mount Moriah, Isaac experiences a deep understanding of God's sovereignty.[15] Esau, upon discovering that his blessing has been given away, learns that Isaac's words cannot be undone. Esau's behavior underscores why God chose Jacob for the covenant line. Though Jacob is a trickster, Esau's profane nature disqualifies him from the blessing.

The Danger of Fratricide

Esau's reaction to Jacob's deception is fury. He plans to kill Jacob after Isaac's death. Rebekah, fearing that Esau might act on this intent and then face retribution, would lose both sons in the aftermath. To prevent this, she persuades Isaac to send Jacob to her family in Paddan-aram under the pretense of finding a wife, avoiding any mention of Esau's murderous intentions. This mirrors Isaac's own journey to find Rebekah, and it sets the stage for Jacob's role in expanding the covenant. From this point on, Jacob becomes the central figure of Genesis, his life occupying 25 chapters.[16]

In Chapter 28, Jacob flees for his life. In verses 3–4, Isaac finally bestows the proper blessing, which includes fruitfulness, numerous descendants, the promised land, and, most importantly, the covenant blessing of Abraham.[17]

This moment effectively closes the narrative of Isaac and Rebekah. A brief postscript concerns Esau: seeing that Jacob's blessing was tied to marrying outside Canaanite circles, Esau marries women from Ishmael's family. In doing so, Esau distances himself further from the covenant line.[18]

CHAPTER EIGHT
Jacob

The last time we saw Jacob was fleeing for his life. However, his life will occupy half of the fifty chapters of Genesis. We have already been present at his birth and early life. We will be present at his wedding, the birth of his children, the death of his wives, and the disappearance of his favorite son.[1] Having stolen Esau's blessing, fratricide was a real possibility. As Jacob travels, he stops for the night. *"He came to a certain place and spent the night there, because the sun had set; and he took one of the stones of the place and put it under his head, and lay down in that place. He had a dream, and behold, a ladder was set on the earth with its top reaching to heaven; and behold, the angels of God were ascending and descending on it. And behold, the LORD stood above it and said, "I am the LORD, the God of your father Abraham and the God of Isaac; the land on which you lie, I will give it to you and to your descendants.'Your descendants will also be like the dust of the earth, and you will spread out to the west and to the east and to the north and to the south; and in you and in your descendants shall all the families of the earth be blessed. Behold,*

I am with you and will keep you wherever you go, and will bring you back to this land; for I will not leave you until I have done what I have promised you'" (Gen.28:11-15). If we go back to the Tower of Babel, the word used for "ladder" in Jacob's dream is the same word used for the stairs of the ziggurat. Jacob, no doubt, would have associated this with a portal between two worlds and would have considered the place a sacred spot.[2] This is not the only place we encounter such a dream. In John, when Nathanael meets Jesus and proclaims Jesus to be the "Son of God," Jesus says, *"Truly, truly, I say to you, you will see the heavens opened and the angels of God ascending and descending on the Son of Man"* (John 1:51). Jacob names the place Bethel or "House of God," and he makes a vow to God.

In Chapter 29, Jacob arrives in Haran, and an interesting detail emerges when you calculate his age: he is 77 years old when he meets Rachel, which is quite advanced for the Ancient Near East.[3] Rachel's name means "ewe lamb."[4] In the ANE, there was a custom requiring that all the flocks gather at the well before the stone covering could be lifted. However, when Jacob sees Rachel, he ignores this custom, lifting the stone on his own like a "he-man," and then waters her flock. Afterward, he kisses her and weeps. This is the only instance in the Bible where a man kisses a woman who is neither his wife nor his mother.[5]

In verse 13, Laban rushes out to meet Jacob, just as he had rushed to meet Abraham's servant a generation earlier. Laban likely hoped for another generous gift similar to the one Abraham had given. After staying with Laban for a month, which probably exhibits the extent of ANE importance of hospitality, the two discuss the terms of Jacob's work, and when the topic of compensation arises, Laban's two daughters are mentioned. Leah, the older of the two, has a name that means "cow" or "weary."[6] Her eyes are described as weak, which suggests she is fragile, tender, or delicate in appearance. Rachel, by contrast, means "ewe lamb."[7] Jacob's choice of Rachel must mean she was especially beautiful. In Western cultures, it is customary for the bride's family to provide a dowry—a payment of money or goods to the groom. However, in the ANE, the groom typically gave money to the bride's family. Jacob, lacking either money or property, finds himself in a difficult position.

In verses 18–20, Jacob agrees to work for seven years in exchange for Rachel's hand in marriage, which may have been a customary form of labor payment in ancient marriage agreements.[8] A typical year's wages were 10 shekels, and the average dowry was 40 shekels, meaning Jacob's commitment represented an unusually generous offer. On the wedding night, however, Laban tricks Jacob by substituting his daughter Leah for Rachel. Leah, veiled, and Jacob, likely intoxicated by the effects of alcohol, explain his failure to recognize the deception.[9]

This incident highlights a pattern of rivalry: just as Jacob and Esau competed for preeminence, Leah and Rachel will compete for Jacob's affection. Leah, longing to be loved, will bear children in hopes of winning his favor, while Rachel, already the object of his love, will yearn for the children she cannot have.[10]

The Trickster is Tricked

After Jacob marries Leah, Laban agrees to give him Rachel as well, in exchange for another seven years of labor. At this point, the tables are turned, and Laban has outwitted the trickster Jacob. In verse 31, Leah conceives. A closer examination of Leah's children reveals that God has indeed honored her. She bears Judah, from whom the kings of Israel will descend, and Levi, from whom the priesthood will emerge. In chapter 30, verse 1, the theme of barrenness resurfaces, this time in Rachel, while Leah remains notably fertile. The rivalry between the two sisters intensifies, and we see repeated exchanges of maidservants, Bilhah and Zilpah, as surrogates for bearing children.

Verses 14–15 highlight a peculiar bargaining episode between Leah and Rachel involving mandrakes—flowers with aphrodisiac properties, known for their provocative appearance and deep roots (Fig. 6).

Later, in verses 22–24, Rachel finally conceives and gives birth to Joseph. By this point, Leah, Rachel, and their maidservants, Bilhah and Zilpah, have borne Jacob ten sons.

At the conclusion of Jacob's additional seven years of service, Laban is eager to keep him and his family around. Jacob, however, strikes a deal for his wages, agreeing to take the speckled, spotted, and black sheep—an arrangement that would typically yield fewer animals since such sheep were rare. Through clever manipulation, Jacob manages to increase his herd, benefiting from the arrangement.[11]

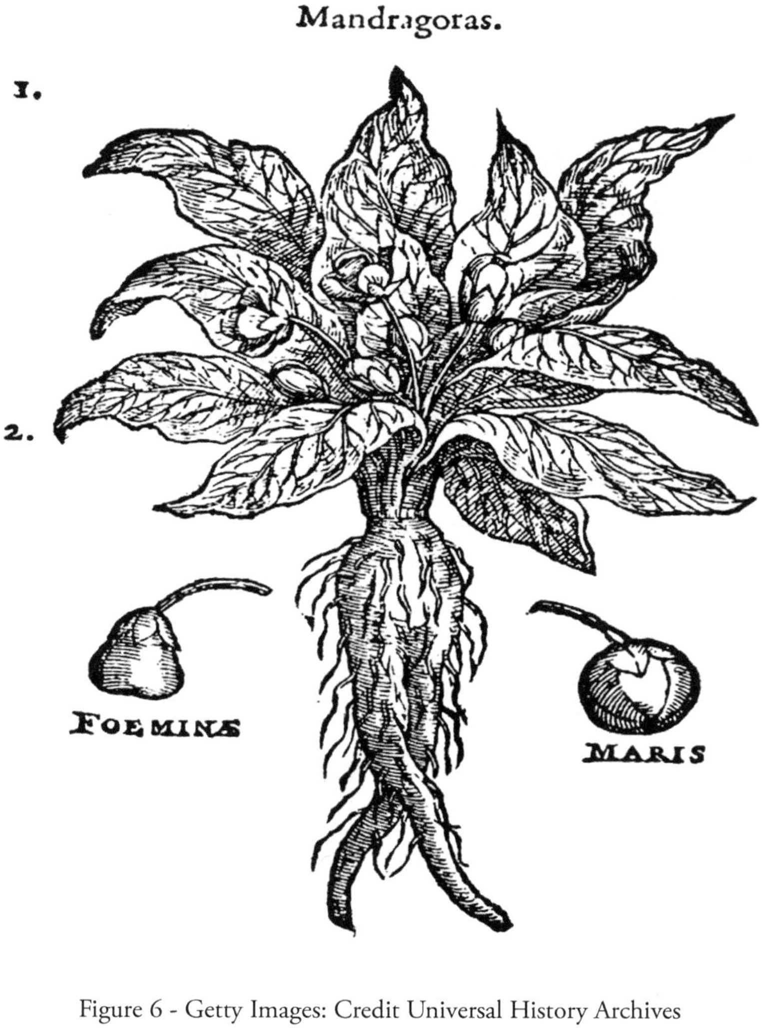

Figure 6 - Getty Images: Credit Universal History Archives

In chapter 31, Jacob recounts to his wives how Laban has cheated him. He reveals that he has heard from the Lord to return to his homeland. In verses 1–7, we read, *"Jacob heard the words of Laban's sons, saying, 'Jacob has taken away all that was our father's, and from what belonged to our father he has made all this wealth.' Jacob noticed that Laban's attitude toward him had changed and was no longer favorable. Then the LORD said to Jacob, 'Return to the land of your fathers and to your relatives, and I will be with you.'"* In verses 14–16, Rachel and Leah respond with a mixture of agreement and complaint. They express irritation that, while Jacob's work has essentially served as their dowry, they have received no direct benefit. As a result, they feel as though they have been treated as foreigners and sold off rather than valued as daughters in their father's household.

Facing Old Problems

As they steal away, verse 19 reveals that Rachel has stolen Laban's household idols. By verse 22, Laban pursues Jacob, but in verse 24, God intervenes, warning Laban in a dream: *"Be careful that you do not speak to Jacob either good or bad."* When Laban finally catches up to Jacob, his initial complaint is not about the idols but about Jacob leaving without giving him a chance to send them off with a farewell celebration. However, by verse 30, Laban accuses Jacob of taking the missing idols.

Jacob, unaware of Rachel's actions, declares, *"The one with whom you find your gods shall not live."* Laban begins a thorough search, eventually reaching Rachel's tent. Rachel has hidden the idols under a blanket and is seated on them. When Laban enters, Rachel excuses herself from standing, claiming she is experiencing her menstrual cycle.

These household gods were often considered family or personal deities. Laban ultimately abandons his search, perhaps apprehensive because of the belief that menstrual blood contains demons. Scholars have long debated Rachel's motivations for stealing the idols and her specific choice of deception. Some argue that she sought to express contempt for her father's gods, while others suggest she intended to undermine Laban as he had deceived Jacob.[12]

In verse 42, Jacob refers to "*the God of my father.*" At this point in the narrative, Jacob views God primarily as a family deity rather than his personal God. This distinction highlights Jacob's imperfect relationship with God, which becomes more personal later in his story.

Before their departure, in verses 43–53, Laban and Jacob establish a covenant to resolve their conflict. They erect a pile of stones as boundary markers and witnesses to their agreement. In the ANE, standing stones often served as guardians of covenants or sacred markers. Here, the two stone piles signify a dual witness: each party calls upon their respective deity as a witness to the covenant. This type of covenant, involving boundary markers and divine witnesses, is of agreements between tribes in the ANE.[13]

As Jacob prepares to reenter Canaan in Chapter 32, the prospect of facing Esau again must weigh heavily on his mind. The chapter opens with Jacob encountering two angels, prompting him to name the place Mahanaim, meaning "two camps." Scholars suggest this name could be prophetic, symbolizing the two camps of Jacob and Esau or Jacob's eventual decision to divide his family into two camps to protect them from total destruction.[14]

Jacob soon learns that Esau is coming to meet him with 400 men, which would represent a considerably threatening force. In verses 3–4, Jacob sends messengers ahead to Esau with a conciliatory message, assuring him that he is not coming to claim any inheritance. In a show of humility, Jacob has the messengers refer to Esau as "my lord" and himself as "your servant." Jacob also instructs the messengers to highlight his prosperity, demonstrating that he has no need to claim anything from Esau.

In verses 9–12, Jacob prays, which is an important moment in the Bible, as this is the first recorded prayer with the actual words spoken to God. In this prayer, Jacob demonstrates great humility, acknowledging his unworthiness of God's steadfast love and faithfulness. He also reminds God of His promises, pouring out his heart in desperation.

To prepare for the meeting with Esau, Jacob sends a series of gifts ahead: ten groups totaling 550 animals, including goats, ewes, rams, camels, cows, bulls, donkeys, and sheep. Each group is instructed to say, *"These belong to your servant Jacob; it is a present sent to my lord Esau."* This act of generosity reflects a profound transformation in Jacob's character—from a grasping, cunning supplanter to a humble and giving servant.

A striking statement appears in verse 24: *"Then Jacob was left alone."* This is the first mention of someone being "alone" since the Garden of Eden. What follows is a night not only pivotal for Jacob but significant for posterity.[15]

In verses 24–32, Jacob wrestles with an angel in what is known as a theophany. A theophany, derived from the Greek words *theos* (God) and *phainein* (to appear), is an appearance of God to human beings, typically revealing something about His character. Though the term itself does not appear in Scripture, the concept is prevalent.[16]

As Jacob wrestles, he seems to be prevailing until God touches his hip and dislocates it. This demonstrates that God could have easily overpowered Jacob but allowed the struggle to unfold for a purpose. Why did God dislocate Jacob's hip? Two possible reasons are often proposed: First, to prevent escape, Jacob would now have to face Esau and confront his own guilt and shame. Secondly, Talionic justice: Rooted in the Noahic covenant and expressed as "an eye for an eye,"[17] this justice reflects God addressing Jacob's history of deceit by dealing with him similarly.

In verse 27, God asks Jacob his name, compelling Jacob to confront his identity. His name, which means "trickster" or "deceiver," symbolizes his past actions. This moment of confession is transformative for Jacob.

Finally, verse 32 offers insight into a later Hebrew dietary practice. It explains that the Israelites refrained from eating the sinew of the hip as a remembrance of this event.[18]

Israel

In verse 28, God changes Jacob's name to Israel, meaning "Struggle with God."[19] This name change is significant, as it demonstrates God's authority over Jacob. In ancient treaties between a suzerain (the more powerful nation) and a vassal (the weaker nation), a suzerain would often rename a vassal to signify control and redefine their identity.[20]

This moment marks a pivotal shift in Jacob's story. While Abraham obeyed God unquestioningly and Isaac did what was necessary, Jacob consistently schemed to achieve his goals. By renaming him, God reshapes Jacob's identity and mission. Israel is no longer just a man but the precursor to a nation. However, this nation is not yet fully formed.

The name "Israel" also reflects the continuing relationship the nation will have with God—one of active engagement and struggle. As someone once described, their relationship with God is like a roller coaster: full of ups and downs, moments of fear and exhilaration, but ultimately secure. This metaphor also resonates with the Christian life, which often feels turbulent but is grounded in God's faithfulness.

In Chapter 33:8, Jacob presents gifts to Esau, a gesture of reconciliation. This act is particularly significant given Jacob's name, which means "he takes by the heel"[21] and implies one who takes. The once grasping and self-serving Jacob is now transformed into a giver. An encounter with God has the power to change us fundamentally, as it did with Jacob.

By verse 18, Jacob purchases land in Shechem. This decision will later lead to disastrous consequences, but it also establishes a foothold in the promised land.

At this point, I will skip over most of Chapters 34–37, addressing these events in the next chapter, titled "The Sons of Jacob." However, Chapter 35 contains an emotional moment as Rachel gives birth to her second son, Benjamin, whose name means "Son of my right hand." Tragically, Rachel dies during childbirth and is buried along the road. Her burial site is separate from the family tomb at Machpelah, where Sarah, Abraham, Isaac, Rebekah, Jacob, and Leah will all be laid to rest.

Rachel's tomb became a sacred site, eventually recognized as one of Judaism's holy places and a destination for Jewish pilgrimage.[22]

From this point forward, Israel (Jacob) begins to diminish in prominence within the narrative. Though his role as a patriarch remains foundational, the focus shifts toward the development of his descendants and the fulfillment of the covenant promises.

CHAPTER NINE
Jacob's Sons

We momentarily shift our focus away from Jacob to an episode that may initially seem out of place but is, in fact, crucial in determining the line of blessing.

Assault and Murder

Yahweh had commanded Jacob to return to his people, yet at the end of chapter 33, Jacob stops short of his journey and purchases a piece of land at Shechem. The text states that he "*camped in the face of the city*."[1] Chapter 34 begins by introducing Jacob's only daughter, Dinah, whose name means "judgment."[2] We read that she *"went out to visit the daughters of the land."*The Hebrew idiom used here suggests more than mere curiosity; it implies a desire to observe, interact with, and form relationships. Notably, she ventures out unprotected. This raises an important question: Why is Dinah among the women of Canaan?

Tragically, Dinah is raped by Shechem, a Canaanite, who then professes love for her. Along with his father, Hamor, he seeks to arrange a marriage between them. In the Ancient Near East, rape was sometimes a precursor to marriage, as later reflected in Deuteronomy 22:28–29, which, in such cases, prescribes a bride price of fifty shekels and forbids the man from ever divorcing the woman. When Hamor appeals to Jacob and his sons, it is the sons—not Jacob—who respond. Jacob's silence is striking. Why does he not intervene? Hamor's proposal would offer Jacob significant economic and social benefits, strengthening his position in the land. However, Simeon and Levi, Dinah's brothers, deceitfully agree to the marriage arrangement on the condition that all the men of Shechem undergo circumcision. When the Shechemites comply and are weakened from the procedure, Simeon and Levi slaughter them all. While their actions might seem like an act of justice, they do not limit their vengeance to the guilty. Instead, they kill indiscriminately, plunder the city, and enslave the women.

Throughout Genesis, the idea of merging with the Canaanites has been strictly prohibited. In this instance, Simeon and Levi may have been right to oppose intermarriage, but their motives—revenge—and their methods—deception and mass slaughter—were profoundly wrong.[3]

Jacob's response in verse 30 is also telling. He uses the first-person pronoun eight times, revealing his primary concern: not Dinah's violation but the potential repercussions on his own safety and status.[4] Leon Kass makes an intriguing observation. He says,

> *We find it hard to square morally the defense of one's own women with the seizure of one's enemy's women. At the same time, however, we are also moved by the suggestion that a community that will make war to defend the virtue of its women, against a community that dishonors other people's women, proves itself—by this very fact of its willingness to fight and die for its daughters and sisters—to be not only more fit to survive and flourish but also superior in justice of retribution is not enough or entirely just, ignoring the matter or doing nothing would seem to be much worse.*[5]

Simeon and Levi justify their actions by arguing that had they not intervened, it would have been as if they had allowed their sister to be treated as a harlot—essentially giving consent to her violation.

As Jacob prepares to leave for Bethel, he commands his household to rid themselves of their idols, making a decisive break from foreign gods and cultures. This act signifies a renewed commitment to Yahweh.

In verse 16, Rachel gives birth to her second son but dies in the process. Before passing, she names him Ben-oni, a name that reflects her suffering. However, Jacob renames the child Benjamin, meaning "son of my right hand," a title associated with strength and protection.[6] Unlike other patriarchs and matriarchs, Rachel is not buried in the ancestral tomb with

Abraham, Isaac, Jacob, and Rebekah. Instead, her burial site later becomes a significant location for Jewish pilgrimages.[7]

Stealing the Blessing

Verse 22 presents another shocking event: *"Reuben went and lay with Bilhah, his father's concubine, and Israel heard of it."* As the firstborn, Reuben stood to inherit his father's concubines upon Jacob's death. By taking Bilhah prematurely, he was making a bold power play, asserting dominance over his father's household. In Ancient Near Eastern culture, such an act symbolized a direct challenge to leadership—effectively a symbolic form of patricide.[8] However, unlike later instances in Scripture where such a challenge might lead to immediate consequences, Jacob does not act against Reuben at this moment. Nevertheless, this offense will ultimately cost Reuben dearly, stripping him of his birthright.

Chapter 36 provides the genealogy of Esau, which holds significant importance for two reasons. First, it demonstrates Yahweh's faithfulness in fulfilling His promise to make Esau into a great nation. Second, it introduces key figures who will later impact Israel's history. In verse 16, we encounter the name *Amalek.* When Israel emerges from Egyptian bondage, the Amalekites will attack them, an act of betrayal that will lead Yahweh to decree their eventual destruction. In contrast, Yahweh instructs Moses not to harm the Moabites, as they too are family, but unlike the Amalekites, they had not acted disloyally.

Verses 23–26 list the twelve sons of Israel. While these sons will form the twelve tribes of Israel, the arrangement presented here is not the final tribal structure. Chapter 37 shifts the narrative focus to Joseph. He is his father's undisputed favorite, and Jacob demonstrates this by giving him a many-colored coat. This gift is more than a display of affection; it is a symbol of Joseph's elevation as the heir apparent.[9] However, Joseph does not endear himself to his brothers. Verse 2 describes him as a tattletale, bringing reports of his brothers' misconduct to Israel. Joseph clearly did not attend the *Andrew Carnegie School of How to Win Friends and Influence People.*

In verses 5–8, Joseph shares a dream in which his brothers' sheaves bow down to his. This vision is intriguing because, as shepherds rather than farmers, the imagery seems unusual.[10] Nevertheless, the dream's meaning is clear, and it enrages his brothers, as it suggests they will one day bow before him.

In verses 9–11, Joseph has a second dream, escalating the imagery. This time, the sun, moon, and eleven stars bow to him—an even bolder vision that implies not only his brothers but also his father will be subject to him. Even Jacob, though initially rebuking Joseph, takes note of the dream's significance.

In verse 12, Jacob sends Joseph to check on his brothers. One can imagine that Joseph relished this assignment, as it provided him with another opportunity to observe—and perhaps report on—their actions. However, in verses 18–32, the brothers, consumed by resentment, conspired against him. Initially, they plan to kill him and present his bloodied coat to their father as evidence of his death.

Reuben, however, intervenes. Rather than allow Joseph to be murdered, he persuades them to throw him into an empty well, intending to rescue him later. As the eldest, Reuben assumes a degree of responsibility for Joseph, as he should.[11] Unfortunately, while he is away, the brothers sell Joseph to a caravan of Ishmaelites, who take him to Egypt as a slave. At this moment, Joseph is only seventeen years old.

Judah and Tamar

Chapter 38 serves as an interlude in the narrative, shifting the focus to Judah. He departs from his family—perhaps out of guilt or disillusionment over what they did to Joseph, though he himself was complicit. In verse 2, we learn that he marries a Canaanite woman, a choice that signals poor judgment. From this union, three sons are born. In time, his eldest son, Er, marries another Canaanite woman, Tamar. However, the Bible tells us that Er was wicked, and as a result, God put him to death. Following custom, Judah instructs his second son, Onan, to fulfill his duty by fathering a child with Tamar on his brother's behalf. This is known as the levirate law.

> *Levirate marriage (yibbum) is the obligation of a surviving brother to marry the widow of his brother if he dies without having sired children (Deuteronomy 25:5-6). The corollary is that the widow must marry a brother-in-law rather than anyone outside the family. The oldest of the surviving brothers had the first obligation to per-*

form this commandment, which also allowed him to inherit all of his dead brother's property.

The explicit purpose of this commandment was to have the surviving brother produce an heir to perpetuate the name of his dead brother so that it would not "be blotted out of Israel."

The literal meaning of the biblical text implies that the firstborn child of a levirate marriage would be named after the dead brother to carry on his memory. However, this is true only in the spiritual sense, for there was no requirement to name the newborn son after the dead brother.

The duty of levirate marriage was obligatory only on one who was alive at the time of the death of his childless brother; it did not apply to one born after his brother's death. Furthermore, both brothers must have the same father. If either of these conditions was not fulfilled, the childless widow was immediately free to marry anyone she chose.

The institution of levirate marriage also served to protect the wife. In numerous verses, the Scriptures lumps widows with orphans and strangers as the disenfranchised members of society to whom special kindness must be shown. The situation of a widow without children was especially

> *dire, for she had no one to care for her and provide material support.*
>
> *As an alternative, the surviving brother could perform halitzah ("taking off the shoe") instead of levirate marriage (Deuteronomy 25:9). If the brother-in-law refused to marry the childless widow, she would (in the presence of the elders) take off his shoe– a symbol of mourning, since his failure to perform levirate marriage meant that his brother was now irrevocably dead.*
>
> *She would then spit on the ground in front of him (indicating contempt), declaring that "thus shall be done to the man who will not build up his brother's house" (Deuteronomy 25:9). From then on, the widow was free to marry anyone she chose.*[12]

Judah refuses to give Tamar his youngest son, leaving her without a husband, children, or means of support. In desperation, she disguises herself as a prostitute and deceives Judah into sleeping with her. As a pledge for payment, Judah leaves his seal, its cord, and his staff—items used for signing official documents, much like a modern-day identification card or credit marker.[13]

Later, when Judah learns of Tamar's pregnancy, he demands her execution. However, she produces the seal, cord, and staff, exposing Judah's hypocrisy. Confronted with the truth, he declares in 38:26, *"She is more righteous than I."*

This statement is striking. Why is Tamar considered more righteous than Judah? There are two Hebrew words for righteousness—one refers to strict legal obedience, while the other is relational, meaning acting rightly to preserve a covenant relationship. Tamar, despite the deception, remains faithful to the family, seeking to secure its future. This is a messy situation, but why is this episode included here?

First, the narrative underscores the complications that arise when a Hebrew marries a Canaanite. Judah's failure to act with integrity contrasts with Tamar's determination to uphold family loyalty. Second, this story foreshadows later events in Joseph's narrative. There is also a deep irony in the symbolism: the staff Judah leaves with Tamar as a pledge for payment becomes the instrument of his confession. Yet later, the staff will symbolize Judah's authority to rule the nations.[14]

Finally, Tamar is named in the lineage of Jesus, marking this incident as more than an isolated event. The theme of family loyalty introduced here will reemerge later in the story—especially when Judah, who once betrayed Joseph, faces another test of character in Egypt.

What we have witnessed in the lives of Jacob's sons will have lasting consequences for family dynamics and leadership. But for now, our attention turns to Joseph's fate as a slave in Egypt.

CHAPTER TEN
Joseph

When we last saw Joseph in Chapter 37, his brothers were plotting to kill him. At Judah's suggestion, however, they chose instead to sell him to a caravan of Ishmaelite traders. As Chapter 39 begins, we are immediately struck by the statement that Joseph was "taken down to Egypt." This phrase carries significant theological weight. In Ezekiel 32, Egypt is depicted as being cast down to Sheol, where it is mocked by the dead alongside other fallen nations.[1] Throughout the Bible, Egypt often symbolizes pride and worldly power, and its descent into Sheol serves as a metaphor for the ultimate fate of such arrogance—complete destruction and death. Meanwhile, Joseph's brothers return home, presenting Jacob with his son's bloodstained robe and fabricating a story that Joseph must have been devoured by wild animals. Overcome with grief, Jacob refuses to be comforted.

Joseph is sold to Potiphar, one of Pharaoh's officials. He proves to be an exceptional worker, and in verse 2, we read, "*The Lord was with Joseph.*" Yet, Joseph himself seems unaware of this divine presence. As the chapter unfolds, his success appears to be attributed either to his master's favor or his own abilities.

Verse 6 states that Potiphar *"did not concern himself with anything except the food he ate."* This phrase may have a couple of meanings. First, it could indicate that Potiphar entrusted everything to Joseph except matters related to his own food, possibly due to ritual dietary concerns. Alternatively, some scholars suggest it is a euphemism referring to his wife.[2] Immediately following this statement, verse 6 describes Joseph as "*handsome in form and appearance*," the exact phrasing used to describe Rachel in Genesis 29:17.

Assault and Prison

Verse 7 introduces Potiphar's wife, who becomes infatuated with Joseph. Traditionally, we think of Joseph as innocent, a victim of sexual harassment. However, it is possible that he knowingly played into the situation. Given his favored status in the household, he could have gotten away with an affair with his master's wife. He sees himself as greater than anyone else in the house, and just as he once provoked his brothers' jealousy, he now appears to toy with his master's wife's desire. He even comes to the house when no one else is around, seemingly flaunting himself before her.[3]

Eventually, the situation escalates. One day, Potiphar's wife grabs him, attempting to seduce him. Joseph flees, but she cries out, accusing him of assault. As a result, he is thrown into prison. Given the severity of the charge, one would expect a death sentence. Instead, Potiphar—perhaps reluctant to lose his best servant—places Joseph in the very prison he oversees. It is likely that he even instructed the warden to put Joseph in charge, for once again, Joseph proves to be an exceptional worker.

Despite his misfortune, verse 21 repeats the key theme: *"The Lord was with Joseph."* But is this truly a misfortune? What is happening to Joseph through these trials? To understand his perspective, we must remember the meaning of his earlier dreams. If they were true, Joseph believed they foretold his receiving the firstborn blessing. His ten older brothers would be bypassed, and he would become the heir to the wealth and authority of the clan of Israel. His father's special gift—the coat—had already affirmed this expectation. However, Joseph is still far too arrogant to assume the role and responsibilities of a godly leader.

In Genesis 40:9–23, two of Joseph's fellow prisoners, Pharaoh's cupbearer and baker, have troubling dreams. Joseph, still displaying a measure of superiority, responds, *"Do not interpretations belong to God? Tell them to me, please."* Notably, he uses the term *Elohim*, which can mean either "God" or "gods,"[4] leaving some ambiguity in his statement.

Interpreter of Dreams

Joseph interprets the dreams of his fellow prisoners, and his interpretations come to pass. The baker is executed, while the cupbearer (wine tester) is reinstated. Before the cupbearer is released, Joseph pleads with him to remember him, but he is quickly forgotten.

In Chapter 41, we encounter Pharaoh. Originally, the term *pharaoh* meant "great house,"[5] referring to the royal palace, but over time, it came to denote the king of Egypt. As sovereign, Pharaoh held both civic and religious authority. The Egyptians regarded him as the living Horus and the son of Ra, the powerful sun god who created all things and was central to Egyptian worship. Pharaohs often identified themselves with Ra to reinforce their divine status. As the supreme religious leader, Pharaoh alone appointed priests to serve in his place. Upon his death, he was believed to become Osiris, the god of the underworld and the afterlife, continuing to aid his people beyond the grave. Pharaoh was also the commander-in-chief of the army and the highest judge in the land. The Egyptians viewed him as essential for maintaining *Ma'at*—the principle of cosmic balance, justice, and order personified by the goddess of the same name. The very concept of law in ancient Egypt was inseparable from *Ma'at,* as there was no distinct word for "law" in the Egyptian language; the closest term was *ma'at* itself [6].. As Pharaoh, his word was absolute and shaped the order of society.

One day, Pharaoh had a series of troubling dreams, prompting him to summon his spiritual advisors for interpretation. Egyptian religion was steeped in magic and sorcery, and Pharaoh, as the earthly embodiment of divine power, was deeply committed to its Mystery Babylon-style system of belief. This religious framework was not a mere set of rituals but the very foundation of Egyptian life. Christians today might reflect on the unwavering devotion of these ancient pagans to their faith—even though it was false—as every facet of their existence was shaped by their religious convictions.

Yet, despite his divine status, Pharaoh finds himself unable to interpret his own dreams—an unusual dilemma, since Egyptian belief held that a god-king should inherently understand such visions.[7] Finally, the cupbearer remembers Joseph. Now 30 years old, Joseph has spent 13 years in slavery and imprisonment. What, then, should we think about these dreams?

> *Dreams were considered a means of communication between the gods and humans. The Egyptians believed that during sleep, a person's ba (soul or spirit) could leave the body and interact with the divine realm. As a result, dreams were often seen as prophetic, revealing future events, divine will, or personal destiny. Pharaohs and high officials paid close attention to dreams, believing they could indicate the favor or displeasure of the gods. Inscriptions from temples suggest that priests specialized in dream interpretation. Some dreams were believed to indicate health conditions or the need for purification rituals. Certain medical texts suggest that physicians took dreams into account when diagnosing illnesses. Egyptians sometimes sought divine guidance by sleeping in temples, a practice known as "dream incubation." They hoped for a revealing dream from a god.*[8]

Egyptians viewed dreams as a liminal phenomenon that allowed contact between the living and the beyond.[9] The Egyptians practiced dream incubation, where individuals would sleep in sacred spaces, such as temples, in hopes of receiving divine revelations through their dreams.[10] One of the earliest known dream interpretation texts is the "Ramesside Dream-Book," which provides insights into how dreams were understood and interpreted in ancient Egypt.[11] Overall, dreams held a sacred place in ancient Egyptian culture, serving as a bridge between the human and divine worlds, and were integral to their religious and daily life.

Verse 14 notes that Joseph shaved before appearing before Pharaoh. This likely included shaving his head, a common Egyptian practice that made him look more like an Egyptian than a Hebrew. Egyptians often kept their heads shaved to prevent lice infestations, a detail that will soon become significant.

After years of waiting, Joseph is finally summoned. He interprets Pharaoh's dreams, which depict seven healthy cows devoured by seven emaciated ones, followed by seven full stalks of grain consumed by seven withered stalks. The repetition of the number seven underscores that God is at work in the coming famine.

Joseph advises Pharaoh to establish a policy requiring that 20% of all produce be stored in preparation for the years of scarcity. Impressed by his wisdom, Pharaoh promotes Joseph to the second-highest position in Egypt, appointing him as vizier. He also gives Joseph a new name—*Zaphenath-paneah*—a hybrid Hebrew-Egyptian name meaning either "He who is called" or "The one who knows." Some translations render it as "The god has spoken, and he will live."[12]

From Prison to Prominence

Roland DeVaux describes Joseph's position:

> *This vizier used to report every morning to the Pharaoh and receive his instructions. He saw to the opening of the 'gates of the royal house,' that is, of the various offices of the palace, and then the official day began. All the affairs of the land passed through his hands, all important documents received his seal, all the officials were under his orders. he really governed in the Pharaoh's name and acted for him in his absence. This is obviously the dignity which Joseph exercised, according to Genesis. He had no one above him except Pharaoh, and he was appointed over the whole land of Egypt; he held the royal seal (Gen 41:40-44), and to describe his dignity the Bible says that the Pharaoh 'put him in charge of his house;' he made him, in fact, his master of the palace (Gen 41:40; 45:8).*[13]

As the famine takes hold, Joseph sells grain back to the Egyptians. By the time the famine ends, Pharaoh will own all of

Egypt, including its land and people. Given Joseph's position as second-in-command, we might wonder where Potiphar ranks in this new hierarchy. This moment would seem like a perfect opportunity for Joseph to seek revenge, yet the text remains silent on the matter.

In Chapter 42, Joseph's long-awaited dream is fulfilled. By now, he is likely 39 or 40 years old, meaning his dream has taken decades to come true. Back in Canaan, the famine strikes, forcing Jacob to send his sons to Egypt to buy grain. By this time, Judah has rejoined the family, but Jacob refuses to send Benjamin, fearing for his safety.

When the brothers arrive in Egypt, verse 6 tells us that they bow before Joseph. However, they do not recognize him. He is now known as *Zaphenath-paneah*, dressed as an Egyptian, and does not speak directly to those seeking grain. Instead, he questions them through an interpreter and accuses them of being spies. In an effort to prove their innocence, the brothers reveal details about their family, including their father and youngest brother, Benjamin.

Joseph then imprisons them for three days. On the third day, he offers them a way to prove their honesty: they must return home and bring Benjamin back with them. In verse 22, the brothers, believing Joseph to be an Egyptian who does not understand their language, speak openly among themselves. Reuben laments, *"Did I not tell you, 'Do not sin against the boy'? But you would not listen. Now comes the reckoning for his blood."* He interprets their current suffering as divine punishment for what they did to Joseph.

The Plot Thickens

Joseph orders that nine of the brothers return home with grain to sustain their family while one—Simeon—is kept as a hostage. Unbeknownst to them, Joseph also has their silver secretly returned in their sacks. When they stop along the way to feed their animals, they discover the money and are both amazed and terrified, realizing they could now be accused of theft.

In Chapter 43, after the family consumes all their grain, Jacob instructs his sons to return to Egypt for more. However, when the necessity of bringing Benjamin arises, he refuses. Judah insists on the futility of going without him, reminding Jacob, *"The man said to us, 'You will not see my face unless your brother is with you.'"* This phrase, *"You will not see my face,"* means they would not be permitted into Joseph's presence—effectively a death sentence for their family, as they would be unable to secure food.[14]

In verses 8–10, Judah takes personal responsibility for Benjamin's safety. Having lost two sons himself, he understands the gravity of such a loss. Reluctantly, Jacob agrees, and the brothers return to Egypt with Benjamin. Upon their arrival, Joseph arranges for them to dine at his house, a surprising gesture that likely fills them with confusion and fear. His steward, a trusted official, oversees the banquet. In the Ancient Near East, such stewards often acted as intermediaries, someone to whom supplicants could appeal on their master's behalf.[15]

During the meal, Joseph inquires about their father, asking whether he is still alive. Perhaps he wonders if Jacob's death is the reason Benjamin was permitted to come, or if his father willingly allowed him to travel. The brothers bow before Joseph again, performing the customary act of obeisance in the ancient Near East—prostrating themselves on the ground.[16]

In verse 30, Joseph is overwhelmed with emotion upon seeing Benjamin. Overcome with compassion, he leaves the room to weep. Leon Kass notes, "Joseph's tears are, the text makes clear, born of compassion or pity, based on brotherly identification. Rachamim, usually translated as 'mercy' or 'compassion,' originally meant 'brotherly feeling' (or 'motherly feeling'), deriving from rechem, 'womb'—itself from a root meaning 'soft.'"[17]

When Joseph returns, he eats separately from the Hebrews, as Egyptians considered shepherds a lower class of people. In their worldview, all non-Egyptians were regarded as barbarians. In verse 33, Joseph seats his brothers in order of age, an astonishing detail that baffles them. When food is served, Benjamin receives five times as much as the others, further increasing their unease.

Chapter 44 will further Joseph's plot. Robert Sacks says,

> *Joseph has now decided to put his brothers to the fullest test. He will place them in a position where they will be strongly tempted to treat Benjamin as they treated him. The point of Joseph's trial is that repentance is only complete when one knows that if he were placed in the same position, he would not act in the same way he had acted before.*[18]

This episode serves as another test of the brothers' loyalty. Will they abandon Simeon in prison, as they once abandoned Joseph? More significantly, will they now forsake Benjamin, their father's new favorite?

Once again, Joseph has their sacks filled with grain, but this time, he instructs his servants to secretly place his silver cup in Benjamin's bag. This cup would have been used for divination—an ancient practice similar to reading tea leaves today, in which omens were interpreted through the movement of liquid in a cup.[19]

After the brothers depart, Joseph sends his servant to overtake them. Accusing them of theft, he confronts them with the missing cup. Confident of their innocence, the brothers boldly declare, *"With whomever of your servants it is found, let him die, and we also will be my lord's slaves."* However, the servant modifies the terms: *"Now let it also be according to your words; he with whom it is found shall be my slave, and the rest of you shall be innocent."*

In verse 12, the silver cup is discovered in Benjamin's bag. According to the agreed terms, he alone is guilty and must remain a slave to Joseph. The brothers return to the city, their fate uncertain.

The prominence of Judah is subtly foreshadowed here—his name is mentioned first, with the others collectively referred to as *"his brothers."* In verse 15, Joseph implies that he has uncovered their guilt through divination, reinforcing his Egyptian persona as a man of supernatural knowledge. The brothers should have realized that someone of his status would be able to discern the truth.

Once again, Judah interprets their predicament as divine justice for their past sin. In verse 16, he confesses, *"What can we say to my lord? What can we speak? And how can we justify ourselves? God has found out the iniquity of your servants."* Notably, he speaks for all of them, uniting the brothers in their guilt. Yet, they still do not recognize Joseph.

Judah then delivers the longest speech in Genesis—seventeen verses—recounting their previous encounters with Joseph. He emphasizes their father's old age and his deep reluctance to part with Benjamin. He also reveals that Jacob believed Joseph had been devoured by wild beasts, a detail Joseph hears for the first time.

In verse 33, Judah makes an astonishing plea: he offers himself as a substitute, begging Joseph to take him as a slave instead of Benjamin. What a transformation! This is the same Judah who once orchestrated Joseph's sale into slavery and who treated his daughter-in-law with contempt. Now, he is willing to sacrifice himself for his brother. At last, he has demonstrated true family loyalty.

In Chapter 45, Joseph finally reveals his true identity to his brothers. The phrase *"made himself known"* is particularly significant—it is a verb form later used exclusively when God discloses Himself to His prophets.[20]

Overcome with emotion, Joseph breaks down and weeps for the third time. This time, his cries are so loud that they echo throughout Pharaoh's house. His brothers, dumbstruck and terrified, are unable to respond.

In verse 3, Joseph asks, *"Is my father still alive?"* This is more than a simple inquiry about Jacob's well-being. Throughout

Judah's speech, he had referred to *"my father"* eight times, emphasizing his personal connection. Now, Joseph echoes the phrase, asserting his own claim to familial identity. Kass suggests that Joseph's question is not just about whether Jacob is physically alive, but whether he is *alive for Joseph*—does he still hold a place in his father's heart?[21]

At this moment, Joseph reframes their past betrayal. He tells his brothers that what they intended for evil, God intended for good—to bring about salvation. He sends them back to Canaan with gifts and instructions to return with their entire family.

However, Robert Sacks offers a sobering perspective on Joseph's words. "While his statement seems sincere, it reveals a misunderstanding of the broader divine plan. Joseph sees his rise to power as a blessing, yet he fails to grasp that these years of prosperity will eventually lead to four hundred years of slavery for his descendants."[22]

The Family Moves to Egypt

In Chapter 46, the entire family moves to Egypt. Surely, Jacob is both anxious and excited. They stop in Beer-sheba on the way, and Jacob offers a sacrifice, for only the second time, to God. God reassures him to go to Egypt and that He would be with him, and would make a great nation out of him. In verses 8-27, we are given a list of all who went to Egypt, mentioning Joseph's two sons among them, who numbered seventy people.

Genesis 47:7-10 is a strange scene where the aged Israel meets the powerful Pharaoh. There are not just two individuals meeting here, but two nations, one of them embryonic and the other the most powerful nation on earth. Old Israel is at the end of a painful and broken life, and the Pharaoh is a picture of power and majesty. But it is Israel who blesses Pharaoh! The irony is impossible to miss. The hope for the world comes from Israel and not from Egypt. Blessing comes from a decrepit and broken Israel and not from a dominant and strong Egypt.[23]

Verse 20 gives us the effect of the famine upon Egypt, which does not befall Israel. We read, *So Joseph bought all the land of Egypt for Pharaoh, for every Egyptian sold his field, because the famine was severe upon them."* The government acquires all of the land through the forfeiture of debt. Now the Egyptians will be tenant farmers. We know that debt slavery was common throughout the Near East. Sometimes it was a short-term servitude, which could be as little as a day or a few years. Here, it will be perpetual servitude.[24] No doubt, this will not endear Joseph or his family to the Egyptians, which could be some of their motivation for enslaving Israel later.

The land of Goshen was not chosen arbitrarily as the dwelling place for Israel. It was excellent pastureland, ideal for grazing sheep. But just as importantly, it was separate from the main Egyptian population, which held shepherds in low regard. Unlike the Israelites, the Egyptians preferred cattle over sheep and viewed shepherding as an occupation of the lowest class.

This separation would ultimately benefit the Israelites. For the next hundred years or so, they would be left to prosper and multiply far beyond their Egyptian hosts. However, over time, Egyptian jealousy over Israel's preferential treatment and growing prosperity would fuel their eventual persecution and enslavement.

Jacob Blesses His Sons

In verse 31, Joseph's second dream is fulfilled—Israel bows before him. Then, in Chapter 48, verse 5, Israel blesses Joseph's sons, Ephraim and Manasseh, adopting them as his own. Once again, the younger son receives the blessing over the older, a recurring biblical pattern of divine election that carries deep significance. Desmond Alexander points out:

> *Not only does Jacob deliberately give the younger son, Ephraim, the superior blessing (48: 17–20), but Ephraim receives the rights of the first-born that should have gone to his father's oldest brother, Reuben (cf. 1 Chron. 5: 1). This event established the tradition that through the tribe of Ephraim, God would create a royal dynasty. Jacob's blessing of Ephraim influenced later developments, especially the choice of Joshua as a leader and the importance of Shiloh in the tribal region of Ephraim as the location for the central sanctuary. All this changed, however, when God rejected the Ephraimites because of their wrong-doing and chose David as king and Jerusalem as his temple city (Ps. 78: 59–72).*[25]

While Reuben, as the firstborn, is entitled to a double portion of the inheritance, this blessing is instead given to Joseph's sons. This is likely because Joseph is Rachel's firstborn, and Rachel was Jacob's beloved wife.

In Chapter 49, Jacob speaks blessings over his sons. As we know, the firstborn is typically meant to receive the primary blessing, but as we've seen, this doesn't always happen. In fact, other younger sons have received the blessing over the older ones: Isaac over Ishmael, Jacob over Esau, and now Ephraim over Manasseh.

Now, we have 14 sons, but only 12 tribes of Israel. However, the tribe of Levi will later be set apart for the priesthood and, upon entering the Promised Land, will not receive land. Instead, they will be scattered among the other tribes. This brings us to 13 tribes. Joseph receives a double blessing through the adoption of his two sons, Ephraim and Manasseh, which means there will be no distinct tribe of Joseph. The result is now, as we have come to know, 12 tribes.

But the question remains: how does Jacob bless his sons? While Joseph's two sons receive the double blessing, the role of family leader is still unresolved. We might assume that Reuben, as the firstborn, would take on this role, but he does not. Why? Verse 4 gives us the answer: Reuben's actions in Genesis 35:22, where he slept with his father's concubine, disqualified him from leadership.[26]

This leaves Simeon next in line, but neither he nor Levi receives the blessing. In verse 6, we learn that it is because of their violent revenge against the Hivites for the rape of their sister Dinah.

The blessing of family leadership falls to Judah. His blessing is one of power and victory over his enemies, as well as fertility and prosperity. Judah's descendants will have such abundance that they will even wash their clothes in wine. Remember the significance of the staff he left with Tamar? That will become the scepter of the kings of Judah.

In Chapter 50, Jacob dies and is embalmed. This practice was not typical for Israel but rather a ritual closely associated with Egyptian customs. Embalming involved an elaborate procedure performed by trained mortuary priests. The body would be treated with embalming fluids for forty days, and the organs would be removed. This process was rooted in the Egyptian belief that the body had to be preserved to serve as a vessel for the soul after death.[27]

After Jacob's death, the brothers fear that Joseph will seek revenge. They approach him, bowing before him once again, but this time they recognize him. Joseph reassures them with these words in Genesis 50:19-20: "What you meant for harm, God made for good to deliver you from the famine."

Joseph lived to be 110 years old. It will be three hundred years before Israel is mentioned again in Scripture, and this time, a deliverer named Moses will rise to lead them.

APPENDIX

Genesis Uncovered Study Guide: For Small Groups & Sunday School Use

Introduction: Using This Guide

This study guide is designed to accompany *Genesis Uncovered* and help readers engage deeply with the text of Genesis through the lens of cultural context, inductive Bible study, and practical life application. Each section corresponds with a chapter or major narrative unit in Genesis.

Study Guide for Chapter One: Context, Context, Context

Key Themes:

- Scripture is ancient and inspired—written *for* us but not *to* us.
- Understanding cultural context is essential.
- The Bible communicates through high-context language.

- Oral tradition and scribal practice support the reliability of the text.

Discussion Questions:

1. What are some assumptions we often bring to the Bible based on our 21st-century Western mindset?
2. How can understanding the Ancient Near Eastern (ANE) worldview change how we read Genesis?
3. What is the danger of reading modern ideas (e.g., science, democracy) into the biblical text?
4. Why is it important to interpret the Bible through a historical-grammatical and redemptive movement hermeneutic?

Application Points:

- Reflect on your own "cultural river." What modern values or assumptions might you be bringing to your reading of Genesis?
- Commit to reading Genesis with humility, recognizing both the depth of the ancient text and the reliability of God's Word.

Prayer Focus:

Ask God to help you lay aside personal assumptions and to open your eyes to the richness of His Word through ancient eyes.

Study Guide for Chapter Two: Creation

Key Themes

- **God as the Source of Order**: Creation is not about material origins but the purposeful ordering of a functional world.
- **Contrast with Ancient Creation Myths**: Unlike pagan myths involving violence and divine need, Genesis reveals a God who creates out of love and sufficiency.
- **Sacred Space and Divine Presence**: Creation serves as a cosmic temple—a place for God to dwell with His people.
- **Separation and Naming**: God's acts of separating and naming in Genesis establish identity, function, and His sovereignty.
- **Functional Ontology**: In the Hebrew worldview, to "exist" means to have function and purpose, not just material form.
- **Humanity's Role**: Humans are created in God's image to steward and participate in His ordered world.

Discussion Questions

1. Why does the Genesis creation story matter today? How does it shape your understanding of God and humanity?
2. How does Genesis challenge or correct the worldviews presented in other ancient creation myths?

3. The chapter says Genesis answers **why** the world was created, not **how**. Why is that distinction important for people of faith?
4. What does it mean that God brings order out of chaos? Can you think of areas in your own life where you need God's ordering presence?
5. In what ways does understanding creation as "sacred space" change how we view the world around us?
6. What is the significance of God "naming" things in creation? How might that connect to your own identity?
7. How can understanding your purpose in God's ordered world help you live with greater intention and peace?

Application Points

- **Rediscover Purpose**: Reflect on how you were created with a role in God's ordered world. Are you living according to that purpose?
- **Trust in God's Sovereignty**: Even when life feels chaotic, remember that God specializes in bringing order out of disorder.
- **Value God's Creation**: Whether it's the natural world, your body, or others around you, creation is sacred space—treat it with reverence.
- **Live with Intentionality**: Just as God named and assigned functions, consider how you can bring structure and purpose to your time, relationships, and work.

- **Embrace Your New Identity**: As someone named and set apart by God, live out your role as His image-bearer in the world.

Closing Prayer

Father of Creation,

We praise You as the One who brings order out of chaos. You created the world with purpose, beauty, and care—not out of need, but out of love. Thank You for making us in Your image and inviting us into Your sacred space. Help us to see the world and our lives as part of Your divine plan. Teach us to live with purpose, stewarding what You've given us, and trusting in Your sovereignty over the unknown. May Your presence bring order to our hearts today.

In Jesus' name, Amen.

Study Guide for Chapter Three: Mankind

Key Themes

- **Human Dignity and Spirituality**: Humanity is uniquely created in God's image, with His breath—His Spirit—infused into us.
- **Creation as Sacred Space**: Eden was not just a garden but a temple where God and humanity would dwell together.
- **Roles and Relationships**: Men and women were created with distinct but complementary roles, equally bearing God's image.
- **Imago Dei**: Being made in God's image gives us inherent worth, relational capacity, and the calling to reflect His rule in the world.
- **God's Rest and Presence**: The seventh day shows God taking up His rule in creation, not in idleness, but in sovereign governance.
- **Blessing and Purpose**: God's command to be fruitful and multiply is both a mission and a blessing, rooted in divine relationship and service.

Discussion Questions

1. What does it mean to you that God "breathed" life into humanity? How does this shape your sense of worth?
2. How is humanity's role in creation different from the roles given to animals or other parts of creation?

3. Why is it important to understand Genesis 1 and 2 not as contradictory stories but as complementary accounts?
4. How does the Sabbath relate to God's rule and presence? What does it say about your own rest and purpose?
5. In what ways do Adam and Eve represent priestly roles in Eden? How might this affect your view of human responsibility?
6. What are the implications of men and women being equally made in God's image but with distinct functions?
7. How does understanding God's command to "be fruitful and multiply" as a blessing, not a burden, reshape your view of obedience?
8. How does seeing Eden as a temple or sanctuary influence how we think about sacred space today?

Application Points

- **Embrace Your Image-Bearing Role**: Reflect God's character in your relationships, work, and decisions. You were created to reflect Him.
- **See Others Through God's Eyes**: Everyone bears the image of God. Let this truth shape your compassion, justice, and how you treat others.
- **Honor the Sabbath Principle**: Learn to pause, recognize God's rule, and dwell in His presence—not just in worship services, but in daily life.
- **Live Fruitfully, Not Just Successfully**: Focus not

on worldly achievements but on producing lasting spiritual fruit through service, love, and obedience.

- **Value Sacred Space**: Create environments—at home, work, or church—where God's presence is acknowledged and welcomed.
- **Understand Your Purpose**: You were made for relationship with God, not just for labor. You are part of His royal priesthood with a role in His cosmic story.

Closing Prayer

Creator God,

Thank You for forming us in Your image and breathing life into us. We are humbled by the dignity You have given us and the role You've invited us to play in Your creation. Help us to see ourselves and others through Your eyes—as image-bearers with eternal value. Teach us to live fruitfully, love deeply, and walk humbly with You. May our lives reflect Your beauty, Your justice, and Your presence. Help us to rest in You, serve faithfully, and live as stewards of all You've entrusted to us.

In Jesus' name, Amen.

Study Guide for Chapter Four: How Far the Fall

Key Themes

- **Sin as Rebellion and Disruption**: The fall wasn't merely a mistake—it was a deliberate rejection of God's authority and order.
- **Deception and Desire**: The serpent's craftiness lies in deception, appealing to pride, autonomy, and distorted views of God.
- **Consequences of the Fall**: The fall introduced spiritual death, shame, blame-shifting, relational dysfunction, and environmental disorder.
- **Loss of Sacred Space**: Humanity was expelled from Eden, symbolizing a separation from God's presence and purpose.
- **God's Grace in Judgment**: Even in exile, God clothes Adam and Eve, foreshadowing redemption through sacrifice.
- **Hope of Restoration**: Though expelled, God's plan for new creation continues through Christ, who will restore order.

Discussion Questions

1. Why do you think the serpent appeared appealing to Eve rather than threatening?
2. How does the serpent's strategy of deception mirror tactics we still encounter today?

3. What role did pride and desire for independence play in humanity's first sin?
4. How does the fall affect our relationships with God, others, ourselves, and creation?
5. In what ways do you see shame and blame-shifting play out in your own life or culture?
6. What does God's provision of clothing say about His character, even in the face of sin?
7. How does the idea of Eden as sacred space change your understanding of the fall?
8. What hope do we have, even after the fall, according to this chapter?

Application Points

- **Guard Your Heart Against Deception**: Satan's tactics often appeal to our desires and pride. Stay rooted in God's Word to discern truth from lies.
- **Take Responsibility, Not Blame Others**: Like Adam and Eve, we often deflect. Spiritual growth begins with confession, not excuses.
- **Recognize the Ripple Effects of Sin**: Sin is never private—it fractures relationships and disrupts creation. Let that awareness foster humility and repentance.
- **Live in God's Grace**: Even after their sin, God clothed Adam and Eve. Let that remind you that His grace meets you, even in failure.

- **Restore Order Where You Are**: Though we live outside Eden, God still calls us to work with Him to bring order to our lives, homes, and communities.
- **Run to God, Not Away**: When shame tempts you to hide, remember Christ came to restore what was lost—don't run from Him, run to Him.

Closing Prayer

Gracious Father,

Thank You that even in our rebellion, You pursue us with mercy. Like Adam and Eve, we have doubted Your Word, followed our desires, and chosen our own way. We confess our pride and selfishness. But we thank You that You did not leave us in shame. You covered us, clothed us, and prepared the way for redemption through Jesus Christ. Restore our relationship with You. Help us live as agents of Your order in a world that still bears the scars of the fall. May we reflect Your grace and truth in how we live, love, and lead.

In Jesus' name, Amen.

Study Guide for Chapter Five: No Order to Order

Key Themes

- **The Escalation of Sin**: Sin grows from disobedience in Eden to fratricide, vengeance, and widespread violence in early human society.
- **The Heart Behind Worship**: God looks not only at what we offer, but how and why we offer it—highlighting the importance of sincere devotion.
- **Sacred Space and Human Alienation**: Eden's loss represents a deeper separation from God's presence; yet, humanity continually tries to regain it by their own efforts (e.g., Babel).
- **God's Justice and Mercy**: From Cain's mark to the flood and the covenant with Noah, God balances judgment with provision and hope.
- **The Power of Legacy**: Genealogies in Genesis show both the consequences of sin and the continuation of God's redemptive plan through chosen lineages.
- **Human Unity vs. Divine Unity**: Babel shows the difference between man-made unity (based on pride) and true unity found only in relationship with God.
- **God's Eternal Redemption Plan**: Even before the fall, God had planned to redeem humanity through Christ—restoring relationship and order.

Discussion Questions

1. Why do you think God rejected Cain's offering? How does this challenge your understanding of worship?
2. In what ways does sin escalate in Genesis 4–11? What patterns do you notice?
3. What role do genealogies play in the biblical narrative? Why are they more than just lists of names?
4. How do Cain's actions and the story of Babel reflect humanity's desire for significance apart from God?
5. How does the flood represent both judgment and a form of "reset" in God's creation?
6. What does the Noahic covenant teach us about God's justice and mercy?
7. How is God's unity different from the world's definition of unity? How does this shape how we think about community and church?
8. What does it mean that God already had a rescue plan before the fall? How does that influence how you see history and your own life?

Application Points

- **Offer God Your Best**: Like Abel, give from a heart of gratitude, not obligation. Worship begins with sincerity
- **Guard Against Sin's Subtle Growth**: Small compromises can lead to devastating consequences. Stay vigilant in your heart and habits.

- **Trust in God's Justice and Mercy**: Even in judgment, God provides protection and purpose. His justice is always paired with grace.
- **Seek True Unity in Christ**: Don't settle for surface-level consensus—find your unity in God's truth, not in human agreement.
- **Recognize the Sacredness of Human Life**: Every person bears God's image. Respond to injustice with righteous compassion.
- **Hope in God's Plan**: Despite humanity's failures, God's redemptive plan continues. Rest in the knowledge that He is always at work restoring order.
- **Embrace Your Role in the Big Story**: You are part of God's unfolding plan, not just a bystander. Live with purpose, humility, and hope.

Closing Prayer

Heavenly Father,

Thank You for revealing to us both the seriousness of sin and the greatness of Your mercy. From Cain to Babel, we see how deeply broken humanity is—and how much we need Your grace. Forgive us when we offer You less than our best, when we try to build our own name instead of lifting up Yours. Help us trust not in our own efforts to restore order, but in the work of Christ who brings true peace. May we find unity in You alone and live as people of hope in a fractured world. In the name of Jesus, who brings order out of chaos.

In Jesus' name, Amen.

Study Guide for Chapter Six: Abraham

Key Themes

- **God's Redemptive Pivot**: With Abraham, God shifts from general humanity to a specific individual and lineage as the vehicle for blessing the world.
- **Faith in Action**: Abraham's story is a journey marked by obedience through trials, revealing that faith is not abstract but active and costly.
- **Covenant and Calling**: God's covenants with Abraham (grant and suzerain-vassal) form the foundation of biblical theology and Israel's identity.
- **Divine Tests and Encounters**: Abraham's life is shaped by tests that deepen his faith and encounters that reveal more of God's character.
- **Grace and Failure**: Abraham is not perfect—he lies, doubts, and falters—yet God remains faithful to His promises.

- **Hospitality, Justice, and Legacy**: Abraham's hospitality, intercession, and lineage become examples of righteousness and God's plan for the nations.

Discussion Questions

1. What does Abraham's calling in Genesis 12 teach us about stepping into the unknown with God?
2. How do the covenants God makes with Abraham shape the rest of biblical history?
3. Why is the contrast between Isaac (the child of promise) and Ishmael (the child of the flesh) important in understanding faith and grace?
4. What can Abraham's tests (e.g., lying about Sarah, offering Isaac) teach us about spiritual growth?
5. How does the concept of covenant faithfulness (hesed) shape our relationship with God today?
6. Why is Abraham's hospitality toward strangers so significant in biblical context—and today?
7. What do Abraham's failures reveal about God's grace and patience?
8. How do you understand the relationship between obedience and promise in Abraham's story?
9. What does the story of Isaac's marriage show about God's providence and guidance?
10. What aspects of Abraham's life challenge or encourage your own walk with God?

Application Points

- **Step Out in Faith**: God often calls us away from comfort to trust Him for what we cannot see. Obedience may mean leaving behind the familiar.
- **Live as a Sojourner**: Like Abraham, we are citizens of another kingdom. Don't get too attached to temporary things.
- **Trust God's Timing**: God's promises may seem delayed, but He always fulfills them at the right time—often in unexpected ways.
- **Offer Hospitality Generously**: Hospitality can be sacred. Practice kindness to strangers as an act of faith.
- **Don't Fear Failures**: Abraham's missteps didn't disqualify him. God works even through our brokenness when we continue in faith.
- **Value Covenant Loyalty**: God honors loyal hearts. Let your life reflect faithfulness in every relationship—especially your relationship with Him.
- **Let God Define Your Legacy**: Abraham's greatness came not from making a name for himself, but from trusting the One who promised to make his name great.

Closing Prayer

Faithful God,

Thank You for calling us like You called Abraham—not because of our worthiness but because of Your grace. Teach us to trust

You when we can't see the whole path. Help us walk in obedience, even when it's uncomfortable. May our lives be marked by covenant faithfulness, hospitality, and humility. We confess our failures and fears, and we ask that You work through them to shape us into people of faith. Let us be a blessing to others as Abraham was.

In the name of Jesus, the promised Seed, Amen.

Study Guide for Chapter Seven: Isaac

Key Themes

- **God's Faithfulness Through Generations**: The promises made to Abraham continue through Isaac, affirming God's consistent covenantal plan.
- **Divine Choice and Human Response**: God chooses the younger son (Jacob) over the elder (Esau), defying cultural expectations to highlight divine grace.
- **Character and Appetite**: Esau and Isaac are both depicted as men of physical appetites, contrasting

with the spiritual significance of the blessing.

- **The Weight of the Blessing**: The blessing in Genesis is not just a paternal gesture—it is legally binding, spiritually rich, and loaded with covenantal implications.
- **Isaac's Unique Role**: Though less dramatic than Abraham or Jacob, Isaac's life of endurance, conflict, and covenant reaffirms God's promises and brings peace.
- **Conflict Resolution and Covenant**: Isaac's avoidance of confrontation and his covenant with Abimelech reflect a peaceful, trust-based leadership style.

Discussion Questions

1. Why do you think the Bible gives relatively little attention to Isaac compared to Abraham and Jacob?
2. How does God's choice of Jacob over Esau reflect His pattern of reversing cultural norms throughout Scripture?
3. In what ways does Esau's impulsiveness serve as a cautionary tale for us today?
4. How does Isaac's deception about Rebekah mirror Abraham's actions? What might this say about family patterns or spiritual growth?
5. What stands out to you about the significance of wells in Isaac's story? How might they symbolize spiritual or relational realities?
6. How do Isaac's blessings to Jacob change from Genesis 27 to Genesis 28? Why is this significant?

7. What role does Rebekah play in ensuring God's will is accomplished? Was her deception justified?
8. What does Isaac's trembling in Genesis 27:33 tell us about his spiritual awakening or realization?
9. How can we distinguish between God's sovereignty and human manipulation in this story?
10. What lessons can be drawn from the way Isaac and Abimelech resolve conflict through covenant?

Application Points

- **Trust in God's Sovereign Choice**: Just as God chose Jacob, He often works through unexpected people. Be open to how God uses those we might overlook.
- **Guard Against Short-Term Desires**: Like Esau, it's easy to trade long-term blessings for temporary gratification. Practice discernment and patience.
- **Pursue Peace Over Power**: Isaac's choice to move rather than fight teaches us the value of humility and trust in God's provision.
- **Take Your Spiritual Inheritance Seriously**: Don't neglect the spiritual blessings passed down through faith. Seek to understand and embrace them fully.
- **Break Unhealthy Patterns**: Isaac mirrored some of Abraham's flaws, but also demonstrated growth. Recognize and work to change unhelpful family or personal patterns.
- **Live with Integrity in Conflict**: When disputes arise, choose peaceful, wise paths. Isaac models how to stand firm without escalating hostility.

- **Honor God's Blessing**: The biblical blessing is powerful. Pray blessing over others with intentionality, knowing God still works through spoken faith.

Closing Prayer

Covenant-Keeping God,

We thank You for Your faithfulness through generations. Even when we falter like Isaac or act rashly like Esau, You remain true to Your promises. Teach us to treasure Your blessing more than our appetites. Help us to walk humbly, to pursue peace, and to recognize Your hand at work in unexpected ways. May we honor the sacred trust You've given us through Christ, and may our lives reflect Your faithfulness to the world.

In Jesus' name, Amen.

Study Guide for Chapter Eight: Jacob

Key Themes

- **Struggle and Transformation**: Jacob's life is marked by wrestling—with others, himself, and God—culminating in a new name and identity: Israel.
- **Grace and Growth Over Time**: Jacob begins as a deceiver but is gradually transformed through trials, encounters with God, and relational reconciliation.
- **God's Presence in Exile**: Even as Jacob flees his homeland, God meets him at Bethel and reaffirms the covenant, showing that divine presence isn't confined to sacred spaces.
- **Family Conflict and Divine Providence**: The rivalry between Jacob, Laban, Leah, and Rachel reveals human dysfunction, yet God's redemptive purposes still unfold.
- **The Danger of Deception**: Jacob, the trickster, is himself deceived, showing the long-term consequences of dishonesty.
- **Personal Faith Journey**: Jacob begins with a borrowed faith ("the God of my father") but gradually develops his own relationship with God.
- **Reconciliation and Redemption**: Jacob's return to Esau and the giving of gifts show how grace transforms takers into givers.

Discussion Questions

1. What does Jacob's dream at Bethel reveal about God's faithfulness even in times of fear and exile?
2. How does Jacob's character contrast with Esau's? In what ways does God use even Jacob's flaws for good?
3. What role does deception play in the lives of Jacob, Laban, and Rachel? How do these patterns affect future generations?
4. Why do you think God allows Jacob to be deceived by Laban? What might Jacob learn from this?
5. In what ways does Jacob grow during his years in Haran? How does his character change?
6. What is the significance of Jacob wrestling with God? How does that event shape his identity and mission?
7. How can struggle with God be a blessing, as it was for Jacob?
8. Why is the name change to "Israel" so important? What does it tell us about God's authority and our identity?
9. What does Jacob's act of reconciliation with Esau teach us about humility and spiritual maturity?
10. How do you see your own life reflected in Jacob's journey—from grasping to giving, from fear to faith?

Application Points

- **Be Honest About Your Identity**: Like Jacob, we all carry flaws and fears. God calls us to face them, not hide from them.

- **God Meets Us in Exile**: You are never too far from God's presence. Even in fear or failure, He draws near with promises and purpose.
- **Expect God to Work Through Imperfection**: God's plan moves forward through imperfect people—take comfort in that truth as you grow.
- **Wrestle with God When You Need To**: Honest prayer and confrontation with God's will can be transformative. Don't be afraid to engage deeply.
- **Let God Name You**: Don't let your past define you. God gives new names and new identities to those who seek Him.
- **Practice Humility and Reconciliation**: Grace turns graspers into givers. Pursue peace with those you've hurt or who have hurt you.
- **Treasure the Journey of Faith**: Jacob's story reminds us that spiritual growth is a process. Keep walking, wrestling, and worshiping.

Closing Prayer

God of Abraham, Isaac, and Jacob,

Thank You that You do not abandon us in our weaknesses. Like Jacob, we often run from our problems, deceive to get our way, or struggle with our past. Yet You still pursue us, speak to us, and transform us. Help us to wrestle honestly with You, to trust Your promises, and to walk in the new identity You give us. May we be known not by our failures, but by our faith in You. And may we, like Jacob, become people who bless others with what we've received.

In Jesus' name, Amen.

Study Guide for Chapter Nine: Jacob's Sons

Key Themes

- **Justice vs. Vengeance**: Simeon and Levi's response to Dinah's assault is excessive and reveals how even righteous anger can turn destructive.
- **Family Dysfunction**: Reuben's sin, Joseph's favoritism, and the conflict among the brothers display deep fractures in Jacob's family.
- **God's Sovereign Choice**: Despite failures, God continues to work through flawed individuals and surprising means—including Tamar—to move His purposes forward.
- **The Cost of Compromise**: Jacob's decision to settle near Shechem results in tragedy, underscoring the danger of partial obedience.
- **Hypocrisy and Repentance**: Judah's transformation begins with his encounter with Tamar, marking a

turning point in his moral development.

- **Foreshadowing Redemption**: The setup for Joseph's future rise is laid through betrayal and suffering, reminding us that God is at work even in dire circumstances.

Discussion Questions

1. Why do you think Jacob remained silent when Dinah was violated? How does his silence contrast with his sons' actions?
2. Were Simeon and Levi justified in taking vengeance on Shechem? How should justice and mercy be balanced?
3. What does Jacob's concern about his own safety in Genesis 34:30 reveal about his priorities at that moment?
4. Why is Rachel's death and burial in a separate location significant in the narrative?
5. What cultural meaning is behind Reuben sleeping with his father's concubine, and what does it teach us about honor and legacy?
6. How does the genealogy of Esau demonstrate God's faithfulness, even to those outside the covenant line?
7. What do Joseph's dreams reveal about his future and the tension they create in his family?
8. How does Judah's relationship with Tamar reflect both his failure and potential for change?
9. Why is Tamar considered "more righteous" than Judah, and what does this reveal about biblical justice?

10. What are the long-term implications of these stories for the future of Israel's tribes?

Application Points

- **Obedience Matters**: Partial obedience, like Jacob's decision to stop short of Bethel, can have unintended and tragic consequences.
- **Let God Handle Justice**: Righteous anger can quickly become unrighteous when we take justice into our own hands. God calls us to act with discernment and humility.
- **Don't Cover Up Sin**: Reuben's and Judah's sins eventually come to light. It's better to repent early than live with compounded consequences.
- **Faithfulness Can Be Messy**: Tamar's story reminds us that God's purposes sometimes unfold in unexpected and uncomfortable ways.
- **God Works Through Imperfect People**: The story of Jacob's sons shows us that God's redemptive plan isn't hindered by human dysfunction.
- **Legacy Is Built Over Time**: Judah begins as a betrayer, but his story isn't over. Neither is ours. God invites us to grow, change, and take responsibility for our choices.
- **Family Choices Matter**: The relational decisions we make today can have a generational impact. Choose faithfulness, humility, and reconciliation.

Closing Prayer

God of justice and mercy,

You see the brokenness in our families, our failures in leadership, and the deep wounds caused by sin. Yet You are never absent, and You never abandon Your purpose. Thank You for working through flawed people to accomplish Your perfect will. Help us to learn from the mistakes of Jacob's sons, to act with integrity like Tamar, and to seek reconciliation when we have caused harm. May our lives reflect Your grace, even in our darkest chapters.

In Jesus' name, Amen.

Study Guide for Chapter Ten: Joseph

Key Themes

- **God's Sovereignty in Adversity**: Joseph's life story is a testament to God's ability to work through betrayal, suffering, and injustice to fulfill His purposes.

- **Transformation through Trials**: Joseph moves from arrogance and entitlement to humility and wisdom through his years in slavery and prison.
- **Divine Providence and Human Agency**: While Joseph's brothers intend evil, God uses their actions for good—demonstrating His redemptive sovereignty.
- **Repentance and Reconciliation**: The emotional reunion between Joseph and his brothers highlights the importance of confession, forgiveness, and family loyalty.
- **God's Presence in Silence**: Though God seems hidden during Joseph's imprisonment, the repeated statement "The Lord was with Joseph" affirms divine accompaniment even in dark seasons.
- **Ethical Growth and Leadership**: Joseph evolves into a model leader—wise, restrained, and generous—prepared to save nations and bless his family.

Discussion Questions

1. In what ways did Joseph's early character flaws contribute to his suffering? How does the text portray his transformation?
2. How is Egypt symbolically portrayed in this chapter, and what theological messages are conveyed through this imagery?
3. What role do dreams play in Joseph's life and in the Egyptian worldview? How does Joseph's interpretation set him apart?

4. Why might Joseph have continued to hide his identity from his brothers for so long? What was he hoping to see or accomplish?
5. What can we learn from Judah's transformation and his willingness to sacrifice himself for Benjamin?
6. Joseph tells his brothers, "What you meant for evil, God meant for good." How does this statement shape your understanding of God's providence in your own life?
7. Why does Jacob bless Ephraim over Manasseh? What does this say about God's pattern of choosing the unexpected?
8. Why is Judah, and not Joseph, given the leadership blessing despite Joseph's role as savior?
9. How does the family's settlement in Goshen set the stage for the book of Exodus?
10. What spiritual truths are highlighted in Joseph's final words and burial request?

Application Points

- **Responding to Injustice**: Like Joseph, we can learn to entrust our pain and mistreatment to God, believing that He works even the worst situations for good.
- **God Shapes Leaders Through Difficulty**: Trials refine us. Our calling may be delayed—but never denied—when we trust God's timing.
- **Forgiveness Is Transformative**: Joseph models how deep wounds can be healed through compassion, humility, and reconciliation.

- **Prepare for Influence with Integrity**: Joseph's leadership was marked by integrity developed in obscurity. God may be preparing you for greater responsibility in your unseen seasons.
- **Faith in the Waiting**: Joseph waited 13 years before his dreams came true. Waiting does not mean God has forgotten; it means God is preparing.
- **Recognize God's Hand in Your Story**: Even when others intend harm, God can weave redemption into your life's narrative.

Prayer Focus

Heavenly Father,

Thank You for the story of Joseph, which teaches us that You are always at work—even in our suffering and confusion. Help us to trust You when life doesn't make sense and to respond to hardship with faith rather than bitterness. Teach us to forgive those who hurt us and to lead with humility and wisdom like Joseph. May we be faithful in both obscurity and influence, always recognizing Your presence with us. Like Joseph, may we see how You use every part of our journey to bring about good. We trust You, Lord, even in the waiting.

In Jesus' Name, Amen.

NOTES

Front Matter

1. Wright, N.T. & Bird, M. (2019). The New Testament in Its World. Zondervan Academic, p. 38.
2. Walton, J. (2010). Covenant: God's Purpose, God's Plan. Zondervan Academic, p. 4.

Chapter One

1. Wesley, John. *Journal*, July 24, 1776.
2. Blizzard, Richard, and Alfredo Garza. "The Evolution and Impact of Archaeological Practices in Biblical Studies." *Bible Scholars*. Accessed March 2024. https://www.biblescholars.org/2024/03/the-evolution-and-impact-of-archaeological-practices-in-biblical-studies.html.
3. Webb, William J. "A Redemptive-Movement Model." In *Four Views on Moving Beyond the Bible to Theology*, edited by Gary T. Meadors, 226. Grand Rapids: Zondervan, 2009. https://faithpulpit.faith.edu/posts/redemptive-movement-hermeneutic.

4. Walton, John H. *The Lost World of the Flood.* Downers Grove, IL: InterVarsity Press, 2018, 24.
5. Walton, John H. *The Lost World of Genesis One and Two.* Downers Grove, IL: InterVarsity Press, 2009, 13.
6. Walton, John H. *The Lost World of Adam and Eve.* Downers Grove, IL: InterVarsity Press, 2015, 15.
7. Walton, John H. *The Lost World of Adam and Eve*, 15.
8. Traffic Report." Accessed n.d. https://www.tagalogtranslate.com/article/example-traffic-report-script-for-radio/.
9. Walton, John H. *The Lost World of Adam and Eve*, 15.
10. Walton, John H. "What is the Ancient Near East?" *Seedbed.* Accessed 2014. https://seedbed.com/what-is-the-ancient-near-east/.
11. Pierce, Larry. "The World: Born in 4004 B.C." *Answers in Genesis*, April 28, 2006. https://answersingenesis.org/bible-timeline/the-world-born-in-4004-bc/?srsltid=AfmBOoqyHzMbfs_oNMfVn0NZY_UlKuEmGbL59u6CwGl_N01nRYl3P38p.
12. Neilsen, 1954. Quoted in Kenneth E. Bailey, "Informal Controlled Oral Tradition and the Synoptic Gospels," *Themelios* 20, no. 2 (1995): 4–11.
13. Hussein, 1932. Quoted in Kenneth E. Bailey, "Informal Controlled Oral Tradition and the Synoptic Gospels," *Themelios* 20, no. 2 (1995): 4–11.
14. Bailey, Kenneth E. "Informal Controlled Oral Tradition and the Synoptic Gospels." *Themelios* 20, no. 2 (1995): 4–11, 5.
15. Bailey, 7.

16. Bailey, 10.
17. Bailey.
18. Bailey.
19. McDowell, Josh. "Meticulous Scribe, Trusted Manuscript." Accessed n.d. https://www.josh.org/meticulous-scribes-trusted-manuscript/.
20. "Ancient Manuscript Comparison Chart." Accessed n.d. https://www.thecollegechurch.org/wp-content/uploads/2016/08/HANDOUTS-Is-Scripture-Reliable.pdf.

Chapter Two

1. John H. Walton, *The Lost World of Genesis One: Ancient Cosmology and the Origins Debate* (Downers Grove, IL: InterVarsity Press, 2009), 20.
2. John H. Walton, *The Lost World of Genesis One*, 40.
3. John H. Walton, *The Lost World of Adam and Eve: Genesis 2–3 and the Human Origins Debate* (Downers Grove, IL: InterVarsity Press, 2015), 28.
4. Leon R. Kass, *Founding God's Nation: Reading Exodus* (New Haven: Yale University Press, 2021), 590.
5. John H. Walton, *The Lost World of Adam and Eve*, 149.
6. Leon R. Kass, *The Beginning of Wisdom: Reading Genesis* (Chicago: University of Chicago Press, 2003), 32.
7. L. Michael Morales, *Who Shall Ascend the Mountain of the Lord? A Biblical Theology of the Book of Leviticus* (Downers Grove, IL: InterVarsity Press, 2015), 49.
8. John H. Walton, *The Lost World of Genesis One*, 26.

9. John H. Walton, *The Lost World of Adam and Eve*, 55.
10. John H. Walton, *The Lost World of Genesis One*, 68.
11. Alexander Desmond, *From Paradise to the Promised Land: An Introduction to the Pentateuch*, 4th ed. (Grand Rapids: Baker Academic, 2022), 12.
12. John H. Walton, *The Lost World of Genesis One*, 57.
13. John H. Walton, *The Lost World of Genesis One*, 59.
14. John H. Walton, *The Lost World of Genesis One*, 64.
15. John H. Walton, *The Lost World of Genesis One*, 66.
16. John H. Walton, *The Lost World of Adam and Eve*, 40.
17. J. Richard Middleton, *The Liberating Image: The Imago Dei in Genesis 1* (Grand Rapids: Brazos Press, 2005), 51.

Chapter Three

1. John H. Walton, *The Lost World of Adam and Eve* (Downers Grove, IL: InterVarsity Press, 2015), 73.
2. John H. Walton, *The Lost World of Adam and Eve* (Downers Grove, IL: InterVarsity Press, 2015), 41.
3. John H. Walton, *The Lost World of Genesis One* (Downers Grove, IL: InterVarsity Press, 2009), 143.
4. Roland de Vaux, *Ancient Israel: Its Life and Institutions* (Grand Rapids: Wm. B. Eerdmans, 1958), 476.
5. John H. Walton, *The Lost World of Genesis One* (Downers Grove, IL: InterVarsity Press, 2009), 72.
6. John H. Walton, *The Lost World of Genesis One* (Downers Grove, IL: InterVarsity Press, 2009), 87–88.
7. John H. Walton, *The Lost World of Adam and Eve* (Downers Grove, IL: InterVarsity Press, 2015), 106.

8. Roland de Vaux, *Ancient Israel: Its Life and Institutions* (Grand Rapids: Wm. B. Eerdmans, 1958), 348.
9. Callahan, S. "Eve." In *International Standard Bible Encyclopedia*, vol. 2, 204. Grand Rapids, MI: Wm. B. Eerdmans Publishing Co., 1982.
10. Reuben Welch, *We Really Do Need Each Other: A Call to Community in the Church* (Glendale, CA: Regal Books, 1990).
11. Catherine L. McDowell, *The Image of God in the Garden of Eden* (Winona Lake, IN: Eisenbrauns, 2015), 138.
12. Catherine L. McDowell, *The Image of God in the Garden of Eden* (Winona Lake, IN: Eisenbrauns, 2015), 78–80.
13. C. F. Keil and F. Delitzsch, *Commentary on the Old Testament: The Pentateuch*, vol. 1 (1861–71; repr., Grand Rapids, MI: Eerdmans, n.d.), 87.
14. Leon R. Kass, *The Beginning of Wisdom: Reading Genesis* (New York: Free Press, 2003), 73.
15. Chiam and Laura, "Hebrew Word Study – Woman," May 1, 2018.
16. Leon R. Kass, *Founding God's Nation: Reading Exodus* (New Haven: Yale University Press, 2021), 592.
17. John H. Walton, Victor H. Matthews, and Mark W. Chavalas, *The IVP Bible Background Commentary: Old Testament* (Downers Grove, IL: InterVarsity Press, 2000), 29.
18. Sandra Richter, "The Ancient Near East and Genesis 2," YouTube video, n.d., https://www.youtube.com/watch?v=-gssQ56kmx8.

19. Catherine L. McDowell, *The Image of God in the Garden of Eden: The Creation of Humankind in Genesis 2:5–3:24 in Light of Mis Pi and Wpt-r Rituals of Mesopotamia and Ancient Egypt*, 2015, https://docs.google.com/document/d/1sScIER6htmbl8ml-iVI208oLg6VPYjmb/edit, 43–44.
20. Sandra Richter, "The Ancient Near East and Genesis 2," YouTube video, n.d., https://www.youtube.com/watch?v=-gssQ56kmx8.
21. Leon R. Kass, *The Beginning of Wisdom: Reading Genesis* (New York: Free Press, 2003), 38.
22. Francis Brown, S. R. Driver, and Charles A. Briggs, *A Hebrew and English Lexicon of the Old Testament* (Oxford: Clarendon Press, 1907), 138.
23. Francis Brown, S. R. Driver, and Charles A. Briggs, *A Hebrew and English Lexicon of the Old Testament* (Oxford: Clarendon Press, 1907), 726.
24. James Hearst, *The Complete Poetry of James Hearst*, edited by Scott Cawelti (Iowa City: University of Iowa Press, 2001), 35.
25. Richard Rohr, *Falling Upward: A Spirituality for the Two Halves of Life* (San Francisco: Jossey-Bass, 2011), xvii.
26. Sandra Richter, "Sacred Space and God's Character in Ancient Israel," July 19, 2020, https://seedbed.com/sacred-space-and-gods-character-in-ancient-israel/.

Chapter Four

1. Polák, J., K. Sedláčková, D. Nácar, E. Landová, and D. Frynta. "Fear the Serpent: A Psychometric Study of Snake Phobia." *Psychiatry Research* 242 (2016): 163–168. As

cited in audiology.org, "Who's Afraid of Snakes?" March 3, 2023. https://www.audiology.org/whos-afraid-of-snakes/.

2. John H. Walton, *The Lost World of Adam and Eve: Genesis 2–3 and the Human Origins Debate*, vol. 1, Kindle ed. (Downers Grove, IL: InterVarsity Press, 2015), 134.
3. J. Julius Scott Jr., *Jewish Backgrounds of the New Testament* (Grand Rapids: Baker Books, 1995), 129.
4. Joseph Soza, *Lucifer, Leviathan, Lilith, and Other Mysterious Creatures of the Bible*, n.d. https://rowman.com/ISBN/9780761868989/Lucifer-Leviathan-Lilith-and-other-Mysterious-Creatures-of-the-Bible.
5. Francis Brown, S. R. Driver, and Charles A. Briggs, *The Brown-Driver-Briggs Hebrew and English Lexicon* (Peabody, MA: Hendrickson, 1996), 791.
6. Francis Brown, S. R. Driver, and Charles A. Briggs, *The Brown-Driver-Briggs Hebrew and English Lexicon* (Peabody, MA: Hendrickson, 1996), 791.
7. R. Laird Harris, Gleason L. Archer Jr., and Bruce K. Waltke, *Theological Wordbook of the Old Testament*, vol. 2 (Chicago: Moody Press, 1980), 671.
8. Adam Clarke, *The Holy Bible, Containing the Old and New Testaments... with a Commentary and Critical Notes*, vol. 1 (New York: T. Mason and G. Lane, 1837), 50.
9. Adam Clarke, *The Holy Bible, Containing the Old and New Testaments... with a Commentary and Critical Notes*, vol. 1 (New York: T. Mason and G. Lane, 1837), 50.
10. Adam Clarke, *The Holy Bible, Containing the Old and New Testaments... with a Commentary and Critical Notes*, vol. 1 (New York: T. Mason and G. Lane, 1837), 50.

11. Leon R. Kass, *The Beginning of Wisdom: Reading Genesis* (Chicago: University of Chicago Press, 2003), 64–65.
12. Noah Webster, *American Dictionary of the English Language* (New York: S. Converse, 1828), s.v. "carnal."
13. Kass, *The Beginning of Wisdom*, 85.
14. Scott, *Jewish Backgrounds of the New Testament*, 129.
15. Ludwig Koehler and Walter Baumgartner, *The Hebrew and Aramaic Lexicon of the Old Testament*, vol. 1 (Leiden: Brill, 1994), 390–91.
16. Kass, *The Beginning of Wisdom*, 82.
17. Walton, *The Lost World of Adam and Eve*, 144.
18. Walton, *The Lost World of Adam and Eve*, 145.
19. Catherine L. McDowell, *The Image of God in the Garden of Eden: The Creation of Humankind in Genesis 2:5–3:24 in Light of the Mis Pi and Wpt-r Rituals of Mesopotamia and Ancient Egypt* (Winona Lake, IN: Eisenbrauns, 2015), 39–40.
20. McDowell, *The Image of God in the Garden of Eden*, 42.
21. Kass, *The Beginning of Wisdom*, 89.
22. Kass, *The Beginning of Wisdom*, 107.
23. Kass, *The Beginning of Wisdom*, 91.
24. Jordan B. Peterson, "Responsibility," YouTube video, n.d., https://www.youtube.com/watch?v=nDDCnMgPnlY&t=3s.
25. T. Desmond Alexander, *From Paradise to the Promised Land: An Introduction to the Pentateuch*, 4th ed. (Grand Rapids: Baker Academic, 2022), 17.
26. Walton, *The Lost World of Adam and Eve*, 158.

27. Dane C. Ortlund, *Gentle and Lowly: The Heart of Christ for Sinners and Sufferers* (Wheaton, IL: Crossway, 2020), 151.
28. L. Michael Morales, *Who Shall Ascend the Mountain of the Lord? A Biblical Theology of the Book of Leviticus* (Downers Grove, IL: InterVarsity Press, 2015), 47.
29. Morales, *Who Shall Ascend the Mountain of the Lord?*, 54–55.
30. Walton, *The Lost World of Adam and Eve*, 150.
31. Kass, *The Beginning of Wisdom*, 117, 119.

Chapter Five

1. L. Michael Morales, citing R. M. Davidson, "Cosmic Metanarrative for the Coming Millennium" (2000), Academia.edu, 112.
2. Leon R. Kass, *The Beginning of Wisdom: Reading Genesis* (Chicago: University of Chicago Press, 2003), 138.
3. Kass, *The Beginning of Wisdom*, 138.
4. Kass, *The Beginning of Wisdom*, 126–28.
5. L. Michael Morales, *Exodus Old and New: A Biblical Theology of Redemption* (Downers Grove, IL: InterVarsity Press, 2020), 107.
6. John W. Hilber, John H. Walton, and Jonathan S. Greer, *Behind the Scenes of the Old Testament: Cultural, Social, and Historical Contexts* (Grand Rapids: Baker Academic, 2018), 393.
7. Roland de Vaux, *Ancient Israel: Its Life and Institutions* (Grand Rapids: Wm. B. Eerdmans, 1960), 4.
8. Kass, *The Beginning of Wisdom*, 144.
9. De Vaux, *Ancient Israel*, 11.

10. Yigal Bloch, “Blood Vengeance in Ancient Near Eastern Context,” *TheTorah.com*, 2022, https://thetorah.com/article/blood-vengeance-in-ancient-near-eastern-context.
11. Morales, *Exodus Old and New*, 10.
12. Stephen G. Dempster, *Dominion and Dynasty: A Biblical Theology of the Hebrew Bible* (Downers Grove, IL: IVP Academic, 2003), 47.
13. Kass, *The Beginning of Wisdom*, 154.
14. Kass, *The Beginning of Wisdom*, 154.
15. EBSCO Research Starters. “Nephilim.” *EBSCO Research Starters*, Religion & Philosophy. Accessed July 3, 2025. EBSCO.
16. . Luther, Martin. *Commentary on Genesis.* Translated by John Lenker. Project Gutenberg eBook, 2010 (originally 1519). In this work (see commentary on Genesis 6:4 and discussion around Joshua 11:7), Luther states that *Nephilim* derives from לפנ, meaning “to fall upon,” referring to violent oppressors rather than giants.
17. Lawson Stone, “Re-Writing Noah: 7 Things You Might Not Know About the Biblical Flood Story,” March 29, 2014. https://docs.google.com/document/d/1bGMb_smh43dVj_56FhHZHRF6zq-h_eCk/edit.
18. Andrew George, trans., *The Epic of Gilgamesh: The Babylonian Epic Poem and Other Texts in Akkadian and Sumerian* (London: Penguin Books, 1999).
19. John H. Walton, *The Lost World of Genesis One: Ancient Cosmology and the Origins Debate* (Downers Grove, IL: InterVarsity Press, 2009), 113–115.

20. Francis Brown, S. R. Driver, and Charles A. Briggs, *The Brown-Driver-Briggs Hebrew and English Lexicon* (Peabody, MA: Hendrickson Publishers, 1996), s.v. "בֶּצַע."
21. Francis Brown, S. R. Driver, and Charles A. Briggs, *The Brown-Driver-Briggs Hebrew and English Lexicon* (Peabody, MA: Hendrickson Publishers, 1996), s.v. "חֵן."
22. Stone, "Re-Writing Noah."
23. Sandra L. Richter, *The Epic of Eden: A Christian Entry into the Old Testament* (Downers Grove, IL: InterVarsity Press, 2008), 57.
24. John H. Walton, *Genesis: The NIV Application Commentary* (Grand Rapids, MI: Zondervan, 2001), 320–332.
25. Kass, *The Beginning of Wisdom*, 191.
26. Catherine L. McDowell, *The Image of God in the Garden of Eden: The Creation of Humankind in Genesis 2:5–3:24 in Light of the Mis Pi and Wpt-r Rituals of Mesopotamia and Ancient Egypt* (Winona Lake, IN: Eisenbrauns, 2015), 122.
27. Leon R. Kass, *Founding God's Nation: Reading Exodus* (New Haven: Yale University Press, 2021), 327.
28. Gordon J. Wenham, *Genesis 1–15*, Word Biblical Commentary, vol. 1 (Waco, TX: Word Books, 1987), 270.
29. T. Desmond Alexander, *From Paradise to the Promised Land: An Introduction to the Pentateuch* (Grand Rapids: Baker Academic, 2022), 20.
30. John H. Walton, *Covenant: God's Purpose, God's Plan*, Kindle ed. (Grand Rapids: Zondervan Academic, 2021).

31. Morales, *Exodus Old and New*, 12.
32. J. Richard Middleton, *The Liberating Image: The Imago Dei in Genesis 1* (Grand Rapids: Brazos Press, 2005), 224–25.
33. Morales, *Exodus Old and New*, 26.
34. Morales, *Exodus Old and New*, 40.
35. Vaughan Roberts, *God's Big Picture: Tracing the Storyline of the Bible* (Grand Rapids: Baker Books, 2002), 47.

Chapter Six

1. Stephen G. Dempster, *Dominion and Dynasty: A Theology of the Hebrew Bible* (Downers Grove, IL: InterVarsity Press, 2003), 76.
2. Dempster, *Dominion and Dynasty*, 77.
3. Dempster, *Dominion and Dynasty*, 76.
4. Leon R. Kass, *The Beginning of Wisdom: Reading Genesis* (Chicago: University of Chicago Press, 2003), 257.
5. "Covenant," *Precept Austin*, accessed [insert access date], https://www.preceptaustin.org.
6. Sandra L. Richter, *The Epic of Eden: A Christian Entry into the Old Testament* (Downers Grove, IL: InterVarsity Press, 2008), 70.
7. Richter, *The Epic of Eden*, 71.
8. Richter, *The Epic of Eden*, 72.
9. John H. Walton, *Covenant: God's Purpose, God's Plan* (Grand Rapids: Zondervan Academic, 2010), Kindle edition, loc. 177.
10. L. W. King, *Babylonian Boundary-Stones and Memorial-Tablets in the British Museum* (London: Oxford University Press, 1912), vi.

11. King, *Babylonian Boundary-Stones*, vi.
12. King, *Babylonian Boundary-Stones*, 60.
13. Moshe Weinfeld, "The Covenant of Grant in the Old Testament and the Ancient Near East," in *The Covenant of Grant and the Abrahamic Covenant*, by Tim Hegg (1989), 185, https://tr-pdf.s3-us-west-2.amazonaws.com/articles/covenant-of-grant-and-the-abrahamic-covenant.pdf.
14. Kass, *The Beginning of Wisdom*, 259.
15. "Alien," *Precept Austin*, accessed [insert access date], https://www.preceptaustin.org.
16. Kass, *The Beginning of Wisdom*, 272.
17. Kass, *The Beginning of Wisdom*, 273.
18. L. Michael Morales, *Who Shall Ascend the Mountain of the Lord? A Biblical Theology of the Book of Leviticus* (Downers Grove, IL: InterVarsity Press, 2020), 27.
19. T. Desmond Alexander, *From Paradise to the Promised Land: An Introduction to the Pentateuch* (Grand Rapids: Baker Academic, 2022), 27.
20. Richter, *The Epic of Eden*, 73.
21. Richter, *The Epic of Eden*, 74–75.
22. Thomas W. Mann, *The Former Prophets* (Eugene, OR: Cascade Books, 2011), 17.
23. Marty Solomon, "Walking the Blood Path," *Covered in His Dust*, June 11, 2013, http://makingtalmidim.blogspot.com/2013/06/walking-bloodpath.html.
24. John Stott, as cited in Vaughan Roberts, *God's Big Picture: Tracing the Storyline of the Bible* (Downers Grove, IL: InterVarsity Press, 2002).
25. Kass, *The Beginning of Wisdom*, 278.

26. Ismar Schorsch, "The Power of Circumcision," *Jewish Theological Seminary*, October 15, 1994, https://www.jtsa.edu/torah/the-power-of-circumcision/.
27. Kass, *The Beginning of Wisdom*, 310.
28. Schorsch, "The Power of Circumcision."
29. Roland de Vaux, *Ancient Israel: Its Life and Institutions* (Grand Rapids: Wm. B. Eerdmans Publishing Co., 1960), 10.
30. Kass, *The Beginning of Wisdom*, 330.
31. Alexander, *From Paradise to the Promised Land*, 35.
32. Kass, *The Beginning of Wisdom*, 350–51.
33. Daniel C. Snell, *Life in the Ancient Near East* (New Haven, CT: Yale University Press, 1997), 55.
34. John H. Walton, Victor H. Matthews, and Mark W. Chavalas, *The IVP Bible Background Commentary: Old Testament* (Downers Grove, IL: IVP Academic, 2000), 55.
35. De Vaux, *Ancient Israel*, 26–28.
36. Walton, Matthews, and Chavalas, *IVP Bible Background Commentary*, 56.
37. De Vaux, *Ancient Israel*, 30.
38. De Vaux, *Ancient Israel*, 34.

Chapter Seven

1. Leon R. Kass, *The Beginning of Wisdom: Reading Genesis* (Chicago: University of Chicago Press, 2003), 474.
2. Trent C. Butler, "Oracles," *Holman Bible Dictionary* (1991), accessed [insert access date], https://www.studylight.org/dictionaries/eng/hbd/o/oracles.html.

3. Iain M. Duguid, *Living in the Grip of Relentless Grace: The Gospel in the Lives of Isaac and Jacob* (Phillipsburg, NJ: P & R Publishing, 2015), 7–8.
4. Tremper Longman III, *Old Testament Essentials: Creation, Conquest, Exile, and Return* (Downers Grove, IL: IVP, 2014), 46.
5. Kass, *The Beginning of Wisdom*, 407.
6. Kass, *The Beginning of Wisdom*, 409.
7. Duguid, *Living in the Grip of Relentless Grace*, 9.
8. Kass, *The Beginning of Wisdom*, 387.
9. Roland de Vaux, *Ancient Israel: Its Life and Institutions* (Grand Rapids: Wm. B. Eerdmans Publishing Co., 1960), 9.
10. Kass, *The Beginning of Wisdom*, 389.
11. John H. Walton, Victor H. Matthews, and Mark W. Chavalas, *The IVP Bible Background Commentary: Old Testament* (Downers Grove, IL: InterVarsity Press, 2000), 59.
12. Longman, *Old Testament Essentials*, 47.
13. Kass, *The Beginning of Wisdom*, 390.
14. Kass, *The Beginning of Wisdom*, 395.
15. Kass, *The Beginning of Wisdom*, 396.
16. Kass, *The Beginning of Wisdom*, 404.
17. Kass, *The Beginning of Wisdom*, 401.
18. Kass, *The Beginning of Wisdom*, 403.

Chapter Eight

1. Leon R. Kass, *The Beginning of Wisdom: Reading Genesis* (Chicago: University of Chicago Press, 2003), 405.
2. John H. Walton, Victor H. Matthews, and Mark W.

Chavalas, *The IVP Bible Background Commentary: Old Testament* (Downers Grove, IL: IVP Academic, 2000), 60.

3. Kass, *The Beginning of Wisdom*, 413.
4. Kass, *The Beginning of Wisdom*, 423.
5. Kass, *The Beginning of Wisdom*, 422.
6. *Brown, Francis, S. R. Driver, and Charles A. Briggs. The Brown-Driver-Briggs Hebrew and English Lexicon.* Peabody, MA: Hendrickson, 2006. Page 528.
7. *Brown, Francis, S. R. Driver, and Charles A. Briggs. The Brown-Driver-Briggs Hebrew and English Lexicon.* Peabody, MA: Hendrickson, 2006. Page 918.
8. Roland de Vaux, *Ancient Israel: Its Life and Institutions* (Grand Rapids: Wm. B. Eerdmans Publishing Co., 1958), 27.
9. Walton, Matthews, and Chavalas, *IVP Bible Background Commentary*, 62.
10. Kass, *The Beginning of Wisdom*, 431.
11. Walton, Matthews, and Chavalas, *IVP Bible Background Commentary*, 63.
12. Kass, *The Beginning of Wisdom*, 439.
13. Walton, Matthews, and Chavalas, *IVP Bible Background Commentary*, 64.
14. Kass, *The Beginning of Wisdom*, 450.
15. Kass, *The Beginning of Wisdom*, 454.
16. Michael Leake, "What Exactly Is a Theophany?" *Bible Study Tools*, July 9, 2021, https://www.biblestudytools.com/bible-study/topical-studies/what-exactly-is-a-theophany.html.
17. Freedman, David Noel, ed. *The Anchor Yale Bible*

Dictionary. Vol. 6. New York: Doubleday, 1992. See entry "Law."

18. Walton, Matthews, and Chavalas, *IVP Bible Background Commentary*, 65.
19. *Brown, Francis, S. R. Driver, and Charles A. Briggs. The Brown-Driver-Briggs Hebrew and English Lexicon.* Peabody, MA: Hendrickson, 2006. Page 975.
20. Walton, Matthews, and Chavalas, *IVP Bible Background Commentary*, 65.
21. *Brown, Francis, S. R. Driver, and Charles A. Briggs. The Brown-Driver-Briggs Hebrew and English Lexicon.* Peabody, MA: Hendrickson, 2006. Page 784.
22. Kass, *The Beginning of Wisdom*, 444.

Chapter Nine

1. Leon R. Kass, *The Beginning of Wisdom: Reading Genesis* (Chicago: University of Chicago Press, 2003), 476.
2. Kass, *The Beginning of Wisdom*, 477.
3. Kass, *The Beginning of Wisdom*, 494.
4. Kass, *The Beginning of Wisdom*, 496.
5. Kass, *The Beginning of Wisdom*, 498.
6. John H. Walton, Victor H. Matthews, and Mark W. Chavalas, *The IVP Bible Background Commentary: Old Testament* (Downers Grove, IL: InterVarsity Press, 2000), 68.
7. Kass, *The Beginning of Wisdom*, 505.
8. Kass, *The Beginning of Wisdom*, 505.
9. Kass, *The Beginning of Wisdom*, 514.
10. Kass, *The Beginning of Wisdom*, 517.

11. L. Michael Morales, *Exodus Old and New: A Biblical Theology of Redemption* (Downers Grove, IL: IVP Academic, 2020), 107.
12. Roy Eisenberg, "Levirate Marriage and Halitzah," *My Jewish Learning*, n.d., https://www.myjewishlearning.com/article/levirate-marriage-and-halitzah/.
13. Walton, Matthews, and Chavalas, *The IVP Bible Background Commentary*, 70.
14. Stephen G. Dempster, *Dominion and Dynasty: A Biblical Theology of the Hebrew Bible* (Downers Grove, IL: IVP Academic, 2003), 90.

Chapter Ten

1. L. Michael Morales, *Who Shall Ascend the Mountain of the Lord? A Biblical Theology of the Book of Leviticus* (Downers Grove, IL: InterVarsity Press, 2015), 80.
2. Leon R. Kass, *The Beginning of Wisdom: Reading Genesis* (Chicago: University of Chicago Press, 2003), 541.
3. Kass, *The Beginning of Wisdom*, 540–48.
4. *Brown, Francis, S. R. Driver, and Charles A. Briggs. The Brown-Driver-Briggs Hebrew and English Lexicon.* Peabody, MA: Hendrickson, 2006. Page 43.
5. *Brown, Francis, S. R. Driver, and Charles A. Briggs..* Page 829.
6. Roland de Vaux, *Ancient Israel: Its Life and Institutions* (Grand Rapids: Wm. B. Eerdmans, 1997), 145.
7. John H. Walton, Victor H. Matthews, and Mark W. Chavalas, *The IVP Bible Background Commentary: Old Testament* (Downers Grove, IL: IVP Academic, 2000), 72.

8. David Falk, "Dreams – Interpretation," *Egypt and the Bible*, February 4, 2019, https://www.egyptandthebible.com/index.php/2019/02/05/dreams-interpretation/.
9. Kasia Szpakowska, "Dreams of Early Ancient Egypt," *Anetody.org*, February 2022.
10. "Languages of Dreaming: Anthropological Approaches to the Study of Dreaming in Other Cultures," in *Dream Images: A Call to Mental Arms*, ed. Jayne Gackenbach and A. Sheikh (Amityville, NY: Baywood, 1991). Retrieved from Wikipedia.
11. *The Dream Book, Google Arts & Culture*, archived October 26, 2016, https://artsandculture.google.com. Retrieved from Wikipedia.
12. Sarna, Nahum M. *Genesis.* JPS Torah Commentary. Philadelphia: Jewish Publication Society, 1989. Page 289.
13. De Vaux, *Ancient Israel*, 130.
14. Sarna, Nahum M. *Genesis.* JPS Torah Commentary. Page 299.
15. Walton, Matthews, and Chavalas, *IVP Bible Background Commentary*, 74.
16. Walton, Matthews, and Chavalas, *IVP Bible Background Commentary*, 74.
17. Kass, *The Beginning of Wisdom*, 589.
18. Kass, *The Beginning of Wisdom*, 591.
19. Walton, Matthews, and Chavalas, *IVP Bible Background Commentary*, 74.
20. Kass, *The Beginning of Wisdom*, 604.
21. Kass, *The Beginning of Wisdom*, 605.
22. Jonathan Sacks, as quoted in Kass, *The Beginning of*

Wisdom, 610.

23. Stephen G. Dempster, *Dominion and Dynasty: A Biblical Theology of the Hebrew Bible* (Downers Grove, IL: IVP Academic, 2003), 89.
24. Walton, Matthews, and Chavalas, *IVP Bible Background Commentary*, 75.
25. T. Desmond Alexander, *From Paradise to the Promised Land: An Introduction to the Pentateuch* (Grand Rapids: Baker Academic, 2022), 52.
26. L. Michael Morales, *Exodus Old and New: A Biblical Theology of Redemption* (Downers Grove, IL: IVP Academic, 2020), 108.
27. Walton, Matthews, and Chavalas, *IVP Bible Background Commentary*, 76.

BIBLIOGRAPHY

Alexander, T. Desmond. *From Paradise to the Promised Land: An Introduction to the Pentateuch*. Grand Rapids: Baker Academic, 2022.

Bailey, Kenneth E. "Informal Controlled Oral Tradition and the Synoptic Gospels." *Themelios* 20, no. 2 (1995).

Bloch, Yigal. "Blood Vengeance in Ancient Near Eastern Context." *TheTorah.com*, 2022. https://thetorah.com/article/blood-vengeance-in-ancient-near-eastern-context.

Brown, Francis, S. R. Driver, and Charles A. Briggs. *The Brown-Driver-Briggs Hebrew and English Lexicon*. Peabody, MA: Hendrickson, 2006.

Butler, Trent C. "Oracles." *Holman Bible Dictionary*, 1991. Accessed [insert access date]. https://www.studylight.org/dictionaries/eng/hbd/o/oracles.html.

Callahan, S. "Eve." In *International Standard Bible Encyclopedia*, vol. 2, 204. Grand Rapids, MI: Wm. B. Eerdmans Publishing Co., 1982.

Chiam and Laura. "Hebrew Word Study – Woman." May 1, 2018.

Clarke, Adam. *Genesis 3: Clarke's Commentary*. https://biblehub.com/commentaries/clarke/genesis/3.htm.

"Covenant." *Precept Austin*. https://www.preceptaustin.org.

Dempster, Stephen G. *Dominion and Dynasty: A Biblical Theology of the Hebrew Bible*. Downers Grove, IL: IVP Academic, 2003.

Duguid, Iain M. *Living in the Grip of Relentless Grace: The Gospel in the Lives of Isaac and Jacob*. Phillipsburg, NJ: P & R Publishing, 2015.

EBSCO Research Starters. "Nephilim." *EBSCO Research Starters, Religion & Philosophy*. Accessed July 3, 2025. EBSCO.

Eisenberg, Roy. "Levirate Marriage and Halitzah." *My Jewish Learning*. n.d. https://www.myjewishlearning.com/article/levirate-marriage-and-halitzah/.

Falk, David. "Dreams – Interpretation." *Egypt and the Bible*, February 4, 2019. https://www.egyptandthebible.com/index.php/2019/02/05/dreams-interpretation/.

Freedman, David Noel, ed. *The Anchor Yale Bible Dictionary*. Vol. 6. New York: Doubleday, 1992.

George, Andrew, trans. *The Epic of Gilgamesh: The Babylonian Epic Poem and Other Texts in Akkadian and Sumerian*. London: Penguin Books, 1999.

Hearst, James. *The Complete Poetry of James Hearst*. Edited by Scott Cawelti. Iowa City: University of Iowa Press, 2001.

Hussein, [author's full name if available]. 1932. Quoted in Kenneth E. Bailey, "Informal Controlled Oral Tradition and the Synoptic Gospels." *Themelios* 20, no. 2 (1995).

Kass, Leon R. *Founding God's Nation: Reading Exodus*. New Haven: Yale University Press, 2021.

———. *The Beginning of Wisdom: Reading Genesis*. Chicago: University of Chicago Press, 2003.

Keil, C. F., and F. Delitzsch. *Commentary on the Old Testament: The Pentateuch*. Vol. 1. 1861–71. Reprint, Grand Rapids, MI: Eerdmans, n.d.

King, L. W. *Babylonian Boundary-Stones and Memorial-Tablets in the British Museum*. London: Oxford University Press, 1912.

Leake, Michael. "What Exactly Is a Theophany?" *Bible Study Tools*, July 9, 2021. https://www.biblestudytools.com/bible-study/topical-studies/what-exactly-is-a-theophany.html.

Longman, Tremper III. *Old Testament Essentials: Creation, Conquest, Exile, and Return*. Downers Grove, IL: IVP, 2014.

Luther, Martin. *Commentary on Genesis*. Translated by John Lenker. Project Gutenberg eBook, 2010 (originally 1519).

Mann, Thomas W. *The Former Prophets*. Eugene, OR: Cascade Books, 2011.

McDowell, Catherine L. *The Image of God in the Garden of Eden: The Creation of Humankind in Genesis 2:5–3:24 in Light of the Mis Pi and Wpt-r Rituals of Mesopotamia and Ancient Egypt*. Winona Lake, IN: Eisenbrauns, 2015.

McDowell, Josh. "Meticulous Scribe, Trusted Manuscript." Accessed n.d. https://www.josh.org/meticulous-scribes-trusted-manuscript/.

Middleton, J. Richard. *The Liberating Image: The Imago Dei in Genesis 1*. Grand Rapids: Brazos Press, 2005.

Morales, L. Michael. *Exodus Old and New: A Biblical Theology of Redemption*. Downers Grove, IL: IVP Academic, 2020.

———. *Who Shall Ascend the Mountain of the Lord? A Biblical Theology of the Book of Leviticus*. Downers Grove, IL: InterVarsity Press, 2015.

Morales, L. Michael, citing R. M. Davidson. "Cosmic Metanarrative for the Coming Millennium" (2000). Academia.edu.

Ortlund, Dane C. *Gentle and Lowly: The Heart of Christ for Sinners and Sufferers*. Wheaton, IL: Crossway, 2020.

Peterson, Jordan B. "Responsibility." *YouTube video*. n.d. https://www.youtube.com/watch?v=nDDCnMgPnlY&t=3s.

Pierce, Larry. "The World: Born in 4004 B.C." *Answers in Genesis*, April 28, 2006. https://answersingenesis.org/bible-timeline/the-world-born-in-4004-bc/?srsltid=AfmBOoqyHzMbfs_oNMfVn0NZY_UlKuEmGbL59u6CwGl_N01nRYl3P38p.

Polák, J., K. Sedláčková, D. Nácar, E. Landová, and D. Frynta. "Fear the Serpent: A Psychometric Study of Snake Phobia." *Psychiatry Research* 242 (2016): 163–168. As cited in audiology.org, "Who's Afraid of Snakes?" March 3, 2023. https://www.audiology.org/whos-afraid-of-snakes/.

Richter, Sandra L. *The Epic of Eden: A Christian Entry into the Old Testament*. Downers Grove, IL: InterVarsity Press, 2008.

———. "Sacred Space and God's Character in Ancient Israel." *Seedbed*, July 19, 2020. https://seedbed.com/sacred-space-and-gods-character-in-ancient-israel/.

———. "The Ancient Near East and Genesis 2." *YouTube video*. n.d. https://www.youtube.com/watch?v=-gssQ56kmx8.

Roberts, Vaughan. *God's Big Picture: Tracing the Storyline of the Bible*. Grand Rapids: Baker Books, 2002.

Rohr, Richard. *Falling Upward: A Spirituality for the Two Halves of Life*. San Francisco: Jossey-Bass, 2011.

Sarna, Nahum M. *Genesis*. JPS Torah Commentary. Philadelphia: Jewish Publication Society, 1989.

Schorsch, Ismar. "The Power of Circumcision." *Jewish Theological Seminary*, October 15, 1994. https://www.jtsa.edu/torah/the-power-of-circumcision/.

Scott, J. Julius Jr. *Jewish Backgrounds of the New Testament*. Grand Rapids: Baker Books, 1995.

Solomon, Marty. "Walking the Blood Path." *Covered in His Dust*, June 11, 2013. http://makingtalmidim.blogspot.com/2013/06/walking-bloodpath.html.

Soza, Joseph. *Lucifer, Leviathan, Lilith, and Other Mysterious Creatures of the Bible*. n.d. https://rowman.com/ISBN/9780761868989/Lucifer-Leviathan-Lilith-and-other-Mysterious-Creatures-of-the-Bible.

Stone, Lawson. "Re-Writing Noah: 7 Things You Might Not Know About the Biblical Flood Story." March 29, 2014. https://docs.google.com/document/d/1bGMb_smh43dVj_56FhHZHRF6zq-h_eCk/edit.

Szpakowska, Kasia. "Dreams of Early Ancient Egypt." *Anetody.org*, February 2022.

Vaux, Roland de. *Ancient Israel: Its Life and Institutions*. Grand Rapids: Wm. B. Eerdmans, 1997.

Walton, John H. *Covenant: God's Purpose, God's Plan*. Kindle ed. Grand Rapids: Zondervan Academic, 2021.

———. *Genesis: The NIV Application Commentary*. Grand Rapids, MI: Zondervan, 2001.

———. *The Lost World of Adam and Eve: Genesis 2–3 and the Human Origins Debate*. Vol. 1. Kindle ed. Downers Grove, IL: InterVarsity Press, 2015.

———. *The Lost World of Genesis One: Ancient Cosmology and the Origins Debate*. Downers Grove, IL: InterVarsity Press, 2009.

———. *The Lost World of the Flood*. Downers Grove, IL: InterVarsity Press, 2018.

———. “What is the Ancient Near East?” *Seedbed*. Accessed 2014. https://seedbed.com/what-is-the-ancient-near-east/.

Walton, John H., Victor H. Matthews, and Mark W. Chavalas. *The IVP Bible Background Commentary: Old Testament*. Downers Grove, IL: IVP Academic, 2000.

Webb, William J. “A Redemptive-Movement Model.” In *Four Views on Moving Beyond the Bible to Theology*, edited by Gary T. Meadors, 226. Grand Rapids: Zondervan, 2009. https://faithpulpit.faith.edu/posts/redemptive-movement-hermeneutic.

Weinfeld, Moshe. “The Covenant of Grant in the Old Testament and the Ancient Near East.” In *The Covenant of Grant and the Abrahamic Covenant*, by Tim Hegg, 185. 1989. https://tr-pdf.s3-us-west-2.amazonaws.com/articles/covenant-of-grant-and-the-abrahamic-covenant.pdf.

Welch, Reuben. *We Really Do Need Each Other: A Call to Community in the Church*. Glendale, CA: Regal Books, 1990.

Wenham, Gordon J. *Genesis 1–15*. Word Biblical Commentary, vol. 1. Waco, TX: Word Books, 1987.

Wesley, John. *Journal*, July 24, 1776.

Wright, N. T., and Michael F. Bird. *The New Testament in Its World*. Grand Rapids: Zondervan Academic, 2019.

ABOUT THE AUTHOR

Michael is married to Barbara, his wife of more than 50 years. They have two daughters, Laura and Pamela, and three grandchildren, Avian, Adria, and Jayna. Michael and Barbara currently live in Oklahoma City. The journey to Oklahoma has been circuitous. After four years in the United States Navy, from 1965-1969, Michael married Barbara, and they lived in the city where Michael grew up; West Palm Beach, Florida. In 1972 Barbara and Michael received Jesus Christ as their Savior while attending the First Church of the Nazarene in West Palm Beach. There, Michael served as youth Sunday

School teacher and Assistant Pastor. In 1979 the family moved to Colorado Springs, Colorado, where Michael attended Nazarene Bible College. Upon graduation in 1982 Michael and Barbara accepted a call to pastor the First Church of the Nazarene, in Covington, Louisiana. Seven years later, they came to the Church of God (Anderson, Ind.), and pastored what came to be known as the Landmark Church of God and Covington Christian Academy. By 1990 Laura and Pamela were attending Mid America Christian University, and in 1994 Michael and Barbara accepted a call to Welcome Home Church of God in West Monroe, Louisiana. After a wonderful ministry of 14 years, Michael and Barbara moved to Oklahoma City. It was here that Michael returned to school at Southwestern Christian University, and earned a bachelor of Leadership degree, and a Masters in Ministry, graduating in 2011. He served as an adjunct instructor for Mid America Christian University from 2010 until 2015. He currently serves as Assistant Professor in the College of Adult and Graduate Studies Christian Ministries, and in the College of Arts and Science School of Ministry.

www.ingramcontent.com/pod-product-compliance
Lightning Source LLC
LaVergne TN
LVHW051225080426
835513LV00016B/1422
9781953285751